TRACKING AND OPPORTUNITY

TRACKING AND OPPORTUNITY

The Locking-Out Process and Beyond

Walter E. Schafer and Carol Olexa
UNIVERSITY OF OREGON

CHANDLER PUBLISHING COMPANY
An Intext Publisher · Scranton / London / Toronto

International Standard Book Number 0-8102-0407-x
Library of Congress Catalog Card No. 70-138517
Printed in the United States of America
Book Designed by R. Keith Richardson

To our children—

Kimberly and Kristin
Julia, Laura, and Michael

—and to all children

Contents

Tables

Appendix: Tables

Preface

That the public schools are failing large numbers of our children and youth is now widely apparent. Precisely why and how, however, are not so clear. To be sure, there is much speculation and criticism based on intuition or experience—some of it sound—about specific effects of schools on students, but there is relatively little systematic evidence. In reshaping existing schools and creating new ones (perhaps they will not be known as "schools" at all), we must know what works and what doesn't in bringing about desired changes in individual students. Toward this end, the concepts, principles, research methods, and logic of the behavioral sciences are increasingly and effectively being employed. At the same time, it has become patently evident that guesswork, hunches, and habit have done untold educational damage, that by themselves they do not and cannot provide a sound basis for educational policy and practice, that they must be supplemented with systematic and rigorous studies of how various school-associated factors affect students.

The attention of both scholars and critics is usually focused on the deleterious effects of two sets of factors: (1) the content of learning (for example, the subject matter is irrelevant to contemporary issues or to the interests and futures of individual students, or it is dull, fragmented, and pedantic); and (2) the structure or process of learning (for example, too much sequencing and scheduling, too little individualization in rate and style of learning, too much passivity by students, and too little social-class and racial mix in the classroom or school).

Employing a behavioral-science perspective, this book represents an attempt to examine some of the effects of one structural variable, the track system, on the behavior and performance of high-school students. The evidence points to the conclusion that the track system is an effective organizational instrument for educational *selection* (that is, screening out), but an ineffective educational *instrument*, at least for students assigned to non-college-preparatory tracks. Bearing in mind the limitations of our sample, design, and data, we suggest from our evidence, first, that the track system is a substantial structural barrier to equality of educational opportunity, especially for large numbers of minority-group and low-income students, who are disproportionately represented on the non-college-prep track; and, second, that the track system inhibits the development of talent and excitement for learning, both of which are so necessary for effective living in the complex, ever-changing world of tomorrow.

While the data from this study identify some of the detrimental effects of tracking, they leave unanswered the question of what the outcomes are likely to be of various alternative organizational models of teaching and learning. More evidence is needed before definite conclusions about tracking can be drawn. But an even greater need is for educational researchers and behavioral scientists to help develop, plan, and test wholly new educational environments. Several general guidelines for alternative models are proposed in the final chapter of this book.

Unfortunately, few behavioral scientists are trained or interested in the methods of planning new approaches or in studying their outcomes—in education or any other field. Those scholars who are socially concerned usually limit their investigations to the nature, distribution, or causes of problems (ourselves included), leaving to "social engineers" the task of developing and testing new models. This fact is deeply rooted in the implicit value system and methodological and theoretical frameworks into which behavioral scientists are professionalized. The pressing need is for entirely new academic roles and graduate training programs that will prepare and support behavioral scientists to help develop and test innovative approaches to educational and other social problems. For example, behavioral scientists might play a vital role in the development of new, more effective educational environments if more of them were trained, not only in the subject matter of their particular discipline, but also in the political, practical, ethical, logical, and methodological skills and knowledge needed to plan new models of teaching and learning, to serve as consultants during their implementation, and to evaluate outcomes. A more detailed discussion of this need is presented in the final chapter.

This book is the outgrowth of the support, encouragement, and stimulation of many people. Most of the data were collected as part of an action-research project with deviant boys. The project was supported by a curriculum-development grant to the School of Social Work of The University of Michigan from the Office of Juvenile Delinquency and Youth Development, Welfare Administration, United States Department of Health, Education and Welfare, in cooperation with the President's Committee on Juvenile Delinquency and Youth Crime. The senior author is deeply indebted and appreciative to the former project directors, Robert D. Vinter and Rosemary C. Sarri, for contributing to the early development of many ideas in the book and for their continuing encouragement. Albert J. Reiss, Jr., also provided stimulation and guidance at early stages and made possible essential support for part of the data analysis through the Center for Research on Social Organization of The University of Michigan. The junior author is particularly indebted for support to the Doctoral Program for Research Training in Behavioral Sciences and Educational Administration at the University of Oregon (United States Office of Education, Title IV, Project No. 061-705). To all participants in the program, faculty and students, we owe a debt of gratitude for inestimable encouragement. We are also grateful for additional support provided by a grant from the Office of Scholarly and Scientific Research of the Graduate School of the University of Oregon. Acknowledgment is also made for the cooperation of the officials in the two school systems from which the data were collected.

Our colleague, Kenneth Polk, has substantially enriched our understanding of the experiences of marginal youth and of how the schools help shape those experiences. We also are grateful for his critical reading of parts of this manuscript. Students in the senior author's seminars on Sociology of Adolescence and Sociology of Education at the University of Oregon have contributed in large measure by raising critical questions about the data and by helping to elaborate and extend our thinking about the interpretation and implications of the findings. Robert Hsieh, Helen Hasenfeld, Robert Thompson, Stuart Wilson, and Gary Hamilton provided essential research assistance in the collection and analysis of the data. The manuscript was ably typed by Jayne Cooper.

Finally, we express our deep thanks to our families for their patience and encouragement during the preparation of the book, and during previous years of study and work.

Jack's Tracks

These are the tracks that Jack built;
They're part of the schools that Jack built.
What happens to kids in the lower track—
That holds them down
And keeps them back?

What does Jack gain by putting them there,
All measured and labeled, and claiming it fair?
Till they see themselves in terms of their track
And stand there shouting,
"I'm all right, Jack!"

C. O.

CHAPTER 1

Tracking and Educational Effectiveness

Several regrettable conclusions about the public schools of the United States are now inescapable. First, equality of educational opportunity for children of different racial and economic backgrounds is more myth than fact. Second, formal education is unsatisfying and unfulfilling—merely something to be endured—for large numbers of young people of all backgrounds. Third, the schools barely tap the intellectual, emotional, and behavioral potential of nearly all youth. Finally, alienation and deviancy among youth, in both individual and group forms, are rapidly rising and can be directly linked to unequal opportunity and to unfulfilling, unenriching, and dull school careers, as well as to other influences.

In short, the schools are falling short in their mission of educating all youth to the fullest possible degree in the self-understanding, knowledge, and skills needed for self-fulfillment, for getting along in today's world, and for constructively helping to create a more humane and livable world for tomorrow. Why are the schools failing? What can be done about it? How can schools better serve the needs of our youth and of our society?

THE SEARCH FOR CAUSES

Any organization's effectiveness or ineffectiveness is the result of a host of interconnected factors: the raw materials being changed, developed, or produced; the organization's social environment and its interactions with that environment; and the programs, processes, or technology used to produce the sought-for outcomes. When an organization falls short of its aims, failure may be attributable to faulty raw materials, to an inhospitable or antagonistic environment, or to a poor program, process, or technology. This general framework is as useful for viewing organizations whose mission is to change people through such means as socialization or rehabilitation as for analyzing factories or businesses.

In trying to understand why schools fall short of their aims, responsibilities, and potentialities, critics of education usually point a finger at one or another of these influences. Many contend, for instance, that the "end product" is faulty because the "raw material" was faulty to begin with: lower-class minority-group youth are not very educable by nature, while school is unrewarding for this generation of middle-class youth simply because they invest so little in it, having become accustomed by affluence and permissiveness to an easy life. Others maintain that the social environment is at fault, that the schools face insurmountable outside barriers: parents who are incompetent or indifferent; neighborhoods plagued with crime, poor housing, and economic deprivation; voters who fail to support budget increases. Still other critics claim that the fundamental problem lies in how schools organize the teaching-learning process, rather than in defective students or outside barriers.

Social science has taught us that behind almost any social fact is a complex web of interconnected causes. This statement is as true of the outcomes of the educational process as it is of the development of achievement motivation or the onset of a campus riot. But recent evidence also makes clear that processes internal to the organization play a far larger role than was attributed earlier in determining the effectiveness of organizations created to socialize, rehabilitate, cure, or otherwise change individuals.

In the case of the schools, it is increasingly evident that there are fundamental defects in policies, programs, and procedures that directly contribute to inequality of opportunity, unsatisfying educational careers, untapped human potential, and deviancy and alienation among youth. In our efforts to reshape existing schools and to create wholly new learning-teaching environments, it is important to understand what these defects are and how they affect the individual student. This book reports evidence on some of the unintended negative effects of one organizational component of many schools: the track system. The following sections of this chapter provide some of the background for our study by briefly reviewing the historical roots of the track system, the educational rationale of the system, some criticisms leveled against it, and the existing evidence about its effects on students.

TRACKING IN PERSPECTIVE

Compulsory Schooling and Pupil Diversity

Since around 1900, United States high schools have experienced a vast increase in enrollment. In 1890, only 6.7 per cent of the high-school-age population was actually enrolled in school, as compared with 94 per cent in 1968 (United States Office of Education, 1969, p. 25[1]). In absolute numbers, this increase constitutes a virtual explosion from 359,949 to 14,200,000. The rapid movement toward almost universal secondary education followed an equally marked trend during the previous half-century toward universal elementary education (Pounds and Bryner, 1967, p. 67).

The reasons for the increased pressures on teenagers to stay in school longer are several: the disappearance of work roles for adolescents, the upgrading of educational requirements for job entry, the declining need for teenagers to contribute to family income, the protection of teenagers from exploitation by employers, and the assumption that an increasing amount of schooling is required for effective participation in today's complex democratic society. Pressures to stay in school were formalized as compulsory-attendance laws, adopted in all states beginning with Massachusetts in 1852 and ending with Mississippi in 1918 (Pounds and Bryner, 1967, p. 67). Interestingly enough, careful analysis of enrollment trends has led some observers to conclude that compulsory-attendance laws tended to follow rather than directly cause increases in enrollment over age 14 (Folger and Nam, 1967, p. 24). Nevertheless, the compulsory-attendance law is the only reason why many students stay in school as long as they do, as reflected in the substantial jump in the dropout rate in every state at the age when attendance is no longer required by law.

Whatever school officials may say about the reasons for compulsory-attendance laws, there is little question that the laws were established and have been maintained more for the benefit of society than for the individual teenager. In a summary of several court decisions which have made this point, the following statement is made:

> In essence the concept is: The purpose of establishing and supporting schools and requiring school attendance is not primarily to benefit the child or the

[1]For complete bibliographical data on works cited in the text, see the References after Chapter 5.

parent. It is for the well-being and safety of the state itself. Its major purpose is the benefit of the society (Peterson, Rossmiller, and Volz, 1969, p. 345).

Many critics have contended that by founding and operating schools on this premise, educators have strayed from the traditional American view that schools ought to serve the interests of the individual first and society second. Paul Goodman, for instance, has remarked that an incompatibility between individual development and national interest would have been unthinkable when Jefferson and Madison conceived of compulsory schooling. To them, being a citizen meant helping to *make* society, not merely adjusting to it. "To make society was their breath of life. But obviously such conceptions are worlds apart from, and diametrically opposed to, our present political reality, where the ground rules and often the score are predetermined," (Goodman, 1962, p. 18).

In the long run, "society" may well pay dearly for holding millions of young people in institutions segregated by age until late adolescence or early adulthood, on one count, because of the immense waste of talent and energy and, on another, because of the "spirit-breaking" often required. Edgar Friedenberg (1965) takes "spirit-breaking" to be one of the principal functions of the school. Society may suffer further because of the resentment developed in large numbers of institutionalized youth toward a "system" that requires them to spend time at tasks which have very little meaning to them—resentment which in recent years is emerging into class-consciousness (by age), class-organization, and class-interested actions, to use neo-Marxist terms.[2]

Perhaps we should withhold judgment. Perhaps society will not suffer at all, but will survive because of compulsory high-school attendance (and its extension, the internalized compulsion to go to college). Perhaps the creative tensions, the pressures for societal change exerted by youth will not be destructive in the long run, but will effect the broad constructive changes hoped for by youth leaders and predicted by Margaret Mead (1970) and others. Perhaps—but we cannot be sure.

Compulsory secondary schooling has had two significant consequences for education, the more obvious being the prodigious number of schools and teachers required during the past century. The

[2]See Dahrendorf (1959) for a neo-Marxist framework that proves to be highly useful in understanding generational conflict.

expansion of facilities and personnel necessitated by a burgeoning population growth has been augmented by the greater proportion of youth staying in school. The second consequence has been the increased diversity and variability of student backgrounds, abilities, and aspirations (Thomas and Thomas, 1965, p. 30). At the turn of the century, only 11 per cent of high-school-age youth was in school, but two-thirds of those who graduated went on to college (Coleman, 1965, p. 5). With increased enrollment, the schools have been faced with a greater proportion of students who are lower in academic ability, achievement motivation, and occupational aspirations. An increasing proportion has come from minority-group and blue-collar homes.

Whereas before the turn of the century a fairly homogeneous curriculum and simple organizational structure sufficed, it became necessary after 1900 to develop a more differentiated curricular and administrative system:

> Starting with 1890, the high school doubled its enrollment each decade through 1930. The high school thus became a "people's college" in which programs of all kinds were set up in order to meet the varying needs of the increased number and range of students (Pounds and Bryner, 1967, p. 68).

The increase in pupil diversity in high schools has also been attributed to the desegregation of the public schools (*Hobson v. Hansen*, 1967, p. 443). Before desegregation, there had been considerable differences in student background, learning rates, and achievement levels between predominantly white schools and predominantly black schools. However, with desegregation in many areas of the country, these differences were increasingly found within the same high school rather than between schools. Most significantly, educators became aware that a disproportionate number of black students were academically deficient and, further, that something had to be done about it.

The Comprehensive School and the Track System

While some of the large cities responded by creating specialized high schools for talented or troublesome youth, most communities developed one or more comprehensive high schools, designed to serve the needs of all adolescents.[3] Some observers have pointed out that in

[3]For details on the history and nature of the comprehensive high school, see Conant (1967), Keller (1955), Hahn (1967), Frankel (1966, 1968), and Levine (1966).

adapting to greater intellectual and motivational differences, comprehensive schools have developed both administrative adjustments among the different classes and grades and a variety of intraclassroom methods of organizing and teaching a range of students (Thomas and Thomas, 1965, p. 97). These writers note that, although not mutually exclusive, the administrative provisions can be separated into several categories (p. 98):

1. Ability grouping
2. Special classes for slow learners
3. Special classes for the gifted
4. Other special classes
5. Ungraded classes
6. Retention and acceleration
7. Frequent promotion plans
8. Contract and unit plans
9. Team teaching
10. Parallel-track plan

Frequently, a school will utilize several of these provisions simultaneously.

It is the last of these, the parallel-track plan (or track system), which is the focus of the present study. An excellent overview of how track systems work is provided in the following:

> A common practice in comprehensive and general high schools is to designate the curriculum according to several fixed areas or tracks, such as college preparatory, vocational, general, etc. . . . Under this multiple track system, the student, with the advice of his counselor, chooses his area of specialized education (college preparatory, vocational, general, business, etc.). But regardless of the specific track a student pursues, there are certain courses, notably English, social studies, mathematics, biology, and physical education, that all students may be required to take. Such universal requirements may be classified as the core or general education sequence, or as constants of the curriculum. In addition to this so-called core or general education sequence, certain electives are offered. Students may be free to elect any course offered by the school or they may be required to select electives from certain fields only. . . .
>
> In some high school programs, students may be required to complete a major and minor sequence. For example, this may consist of two majors of three years each, and two minors of two years each (Tanner, 1965, pp. 221–224). (Reprinted with permission of The Macmillan Company from *Schools for Youth: Change and Challenge in Secondary Education* by Daniel Tanner. Copyright © 1965 by Daniel Tanner.)

Tanner gives an example of a program of studies in a hypothetical track system at a large four-year comprehensive high school (see table). Another variation of the track system is described in *Hobson v. Hansen* (1967, pp. 442–449) as it operated in the public schools in the District of Columbia. The track system included four separate curricular programs: Basic or Special Academic, for slow learners or the academically retarded; General, a terminal program of vocational preparation for students who were not expected to continue their education beyond high-school graduation; Regular, a college-preparatory program for students expected to continue their education at the college level; and Honors, an accelerated program for intellectually gifted students.[4] The criteria used for assigning students to the four tracks in the District of Columbia schools were the same as those used in most high schools with track systems: " . . . aptitude, achievement, teacher recommendations, prior academic record (that is, in junior high school), social maturity, and pupil preferences or interests" (Tanner, 1965, p. 463).

There are several basic assumptions underlying the track system. One of these directly supports the application of these selection criteria: that "a child's maximum educational potential can and will be accurately measured" (*Hobson v. Hansen*, 1967, pp. 443–446). Should this premise prove false, both the theory and its justification fall open to question.

A case study of a Midwestern high school found that judgments by counselors about the "social character" and "adjustment" of students also played an important part in the determination of whether or not the student was "college material" (Cicourel and Kitsuse, 1963). Classroom teachers' opinions are also a primary source of student evaluations leading to track assignment. Theoretically, the student or his parent can overrule the assignment decision made by the counselor or teacher. How often such decisions are overruled remains an open question. Lower-income students or parents no doubt assert themselves in this way least of all:

> Parents, according to printed policy, have always had the right to protest the placement of their children in basic or regular track. Relatively few did, or do, however. Most parents of poverty area pupils would feel themselves incapable of arguing the point, even if they were aware of it (Committee on Education and Labor, 1966, p. 39).

In short, the counselor or teacher has a vital influence on the life career as well as later school career of a student by assigning him to one or another track.

[4]See Hansen (1964), the principal designer and defender of the four-track system, for a detailed description of the theoretical model, its intended function and its underlying rationale.

SAMPLE PROGRAM OF STUDIES IN A LARGE COMPREHENSIVE FOUR-YEAR HIGH SCHOOL

[Reprinted with permission of The Macmillan Company from *Schools for Youth: Change and Challenge in Secondary Education* by Daniel Tanner. Copyright © 1965 by Daniel Tanner.]

Year	*College Preparatory*	*General*	*Practical Arts*	*Vocational Education*	*Business Education*	*Fine Arts*
FRESHMAN* (9th Grade)	English I Social Studies Algebra Physical Educ. Foreign Lang. Elective	English I Social Studies Mathematics Physical Educ. General Science Elective	English I Social Studies Mathematics Physical Educ. Industrial Arts or Homemaking Elective	English I Social Studies Mathematics Physical Educ. Trades & Industs., Vocational Homemaking, or Distrib. Occup. Elective	English I Social Studies Mathematics Physical Educ. General Business Elective	English I Social Studies Mathematics Physical Educ. Art or Music Elective
SOPHOMORE (10th Grade)	English II Biology Physical Educ. Geometry Foreign Lang. Elective	English II Biology Physical Educ. Math or Algebra Elective Elective	English II Biology Physical Educ. Math or Algebra Industrial Arts or Homemaking Elective	English II Biology Physical Educ. Math or Algebra Trades & Industs., Vocational Homemaking, or Distrib. Occup. Elective	English II Biology Physical Educ. Math or Algebra Typing Elective	English II Biology Physical Educ. Math or Algebra Art or Music Elective

JUNIOR (11th Grade)	English III U.S. History Physical Educ. Advanced Alg. Foreign Lang. Elective	English III U.S. History Physical Educ. Elective Elective Elective	English III U.S. History Physical Educ. Industrial Arts or Homemaking Elective Elective	English III U.S. History Physical Educ. Trades & Industs., Vocational Homemaking, or Distrib. Occup. Elective Elective	English III U.S. History Physical Educ. Typing Shorthand or Bookkeeping Elective	English III U.S. History Physical Educ. Art or Music Elective Elective
SENIOR (12th Grade)	English IV American Gov't. Physical Educ. Chemistry or Physics Elective Elective	American Gov't. Physical Educ. Elective Elective Elective Elective	American Gov't. Physical Educ. Industrial Arts or Homemaking Elective Elective Elective	American Gov't. Physical Educ. Trades & Industs., Vocational Homemaking, or Distrib. Occup. Elective Elective Elective	American Gov't. Physical Educ. Shorthand or Bookkeeping Elective Elective Elective	American Gov't. Physical Educ. Art or Music Elective Elective Elective

*School systems with a three-year junior high school and a three-year senior high school (6–3–3), absorb this into the final year of the junior high school.

RATIONALES FOR THE TRACK SYSTEM

Several different rationales are given by schools for track systems. In addition to the assumptions that educational potential will be accurately measured and that students will be assigned appropriately, common to most is the assumption that learning can progress more efficiently and effectively when all members of the instructional group are relatively homogeneous in level of ability and performance. Thus, college-preparatory students, who are considered to be brighter and able to learn more rapidly, are set apart for all or most of the school day in order not to be "held back" by non-college-preparatory students. As we will see later, this assumption may well become self-fulfilling.

While students considered bright are expected to learn more efficiently and effectively when instructed in homogeneous ability groups, those considered dull are also expected to benefit. The track system is expected to enhance the likelihood that the school will be able to remedy the slow or dull student's educational deficiencies. We will examine later whether or not this expected improvement in slow students' educational skills actually takes place within the track system; however, it is important to bear in mind that this constitutes a fundamental assumption underlying the theory of tracking.

Another common element in most official rationales is that the subject matter needed differs for college-bound and non-college-bound students. Whereas the college-bound are thought to need foreign languages and advanced science and mathematics, the non-college-bound are judged to need only "basic" science and mathematics, no foreign languages, but various business, shop, or other vocational courses.

A good summary of the educational rationale for tracking is contained in the following:

> We recommend that beginning with the ninth grade separate, fixed curricula—such as academic, commercial, general, and industrial arts—be established. Students should be held to one of these on the basis partly of achievement, partly of preference and interests, with the possibility of shifting from one curriculum to another according to achievement. Such a system would prevent able students from taking easy courses in order to make high grades with little effort; it would prevent all students from wasting time with dubious or irrelevant electives; and, by reducing programming to a simple routine easily handled by administrative clerks, it would relieve many teachers from counselling and return them to the more important work of teaching. (Curriculum Survey Committee, 1960, p. 10).

CRITICISMS OF THE TRACK SYSTEM

In a fashion all too typical, the tracking system has been adopted, imbedded, and retained by about half of the high schools in the United States—despite the almost total lack of evidence of its positive educational effects. While tracking has unquestionable administrative and management benefits, there is growing concern that these gains are outweighed by much greater costs to students. This concern has been expressed in a number of specific criticisms which warrant brief review as a means of sharpening and directing the focus of our own analysis.

Discrimination in Assignment

One criticism is that the procedures for assigning students to a track at the beginning of high school (or earlier) intentionally or unintentionally discriminate against those from lower-income or minority-group families.[5] One form of this argument is that the tests on which track assignment is based are weighted in favor of white middle-class students. Many tests actually measure verbal skills rather than the intellectual potential for acquiring those skills, and more white middle-class students than minority-group, lower-class students have acquired competence in those skills, partly because of differences in the quality of previous schooling.

Critics further point out that regardless of ability, past performance, or aspirations, the white middle-class student is more likely than the minority-group, lower-income student to be assigned to the college-prep track. This situation may result from direct discrimination by a counselor or teacher, from unintended and unrecognized race or class bias, from differing parental pressures on counselors or teachers, or from different projections of the student's college chances, based on knowledge of the school careers of older siblings or on perceptions of family resources for college.

The organizational processes of curriculum assignment are complex, with assumptions made by counselors about the character, adjustment, and alleged potential of incoming students playing an important part in the decision (Cicourel and Kitsuse, 1963). Whatever the precise dynamics of the process, there is some evidence to support the critics, as we will see.

[5]See, for example, Backman and Secord (1968, p. 80), Pearl (1967, p. 316), and *Hobson v. Hansen* (1967, p. 407).

Inflexibility to Developmental Change

Another criticism is that track systems prematurely lock students into a particular educational and occupational career line.[6] Once having chosen or been assigned to a track, the student has little opportunity for changing later. Students soon internalize the school's formal definition of themselves as "bright" or "not so bright" and become either too intimidated to shift upward or too proud to move down. Another is that many advanced college-preparatory courses require prerequisites that must be taken early in the high-school career. Thus, non-college-preparatory students are automatically barred from moving up to the college-preparatory track, at least without delaying their graduation. For instance, students who have not had algebra as sophomores cannot take calculus as seniors.

It is argued, then, that despite individual differences in psychological, intellectual, and motivational growth, students' chances of qualifying for college (except for open-door colleges)—and hence their life-career chances—are virtually set at age 14 or 15. Such premature and inflexible decisions are inconsistent with the American ideal of "contest mobility," by which the individual has maximum opportunity to move up or down the status hierarchies (Turner, 1960). In broad, humanistic terms, tracking is thought to represent an unfortunate restriction on the freedom of choice and option for the individual student.

Inferior Education

Other critics claim that the education afforded lower-track students is of inferior quality to that of upper-track students.[7] The discrepancy results from low expectations by teachers, damaged self-esteem because of the stigma attached to lower tracks, poor peer models, dull subject matter, and ineffective and uninspired teaching in the lower track. Because lower-income and minority-group students are disproportionately assigned to lower tracks and because the lower tracks are marked by inferior instruction and learning, the chances are substantially reduced that these students will retain an interest in school and experience success there:

[6]See, for example, Venn (1964, p. 32), Tree (1968, p. 11), Backman and Secord (1968, p. 81), Thomas and Thomas (1965, p. 30), Tanner (1965, p. 463), Thelen (1967, p. 30), and *Hobson v. Hansen* (1967, pp. 459–463).

[7]See, for instance, Pearl (1965, 1967), Schafer and Polk (1967, p. 240), Glasser (1969, p. 82), Sexton (1967, p. 58), and *Hobson v. Hansen* (1967, p. 407).

> . . . "special ability classes," "basic track," or "slow learner" classes are various names for another means of systematically denying the poor adequate access to education (Pearl, 1965, p. 92).

Based on his research in Harlem schools, another observer concluded:

> It is conceivable that the detrimental effects of segregation based upon intellect are similar to the known detrimental effects of schools segregated on the basis of class, nationality, or race (K. Clark, 1963, p. 152).

Limited Contact with Other Backgrounds

Another criticism is that, through the economic and racial segregation imposed on the classroom by the track system and through the influence of the track system on friendship patterns, the educational system fails to prepare students for effective living in an open, multiethnic society. Rather, they are led to accept separation along economic and racial lines as normal and acceptable, all the while failing to learn through close daily contact about those from other backgrounds. This argument is based on the assumption that informal friendships are likely to be partly determined and limited by one's track position. Evidence that interracial attitudes and behavior in adulthood are linked to whether the person attended a segregated or an integrated school may well apply to segregation within a school as well (United States Commission on Civil Rights, 1968, p. 161).

Rebellion against the Stigma

Finally, it is sometimes contended that, through tracking, the schools actually contribute to the problems they seek to prevent: rebelliousness, dropping out, and delinquency.[8] As already noted, many critics argue that lower-track students are more likely to fail, become alienated, and develop a pessimistic attitude toward themselves and their future, partly because of the track system itself. Insofar as these factors contribute to deviancy in school, dropping out, and delinquency, the school, through its track system, is said to help generate, rather than deter, youth problems.

This contention is repugnant to those teachers, counselors, and administrators who devote their energy and commit their good will to helping youth. However, the criticism is directed not so much at the performance of individual teachers but at an element of the organization in which they work. Tracking is a system variable, not an in-

[8]See, for example, Schafer and Polk (1967, p. 242), and Pearl (1965, 1967).

dividual variable. Hence, evidence in support of the critics ought to be regarded less as a threat to the competence or performance of the individual schoolman than as a challenge to seek new organizational forms.

THE NEED FOR EVIDENCE

At the beginning of this chapter, we identified four inescapable conclusions about the public schools of the United States: (1) equality of educational opportunity is more myth than fact; (2) school for many is unfulfilling and unsatisfying; (3) the potential for intellectual, emotional, and behavioral growth is barely tapped in most students; and (4) the schools contribute to rebelliousness, discontent, and deviancy. It was pointed out that attention must be directed to processes within the educational system itself in the search for explanations of these realities. Finally, it was noted that, according to numerous critics, the track system is one component of school structure which contributes to these as well as other negative outcomes of schooling.

The view that tracking vitally affects the process and outcome of education is entirely consistent with general social-psychological theory. Tracking is best conceived as a feature of the school as a social organization. Built into it are institutionalized labels, role expectations, behavior patterns, and role relationships. Evidence from a variety of organizational types has led theorists to the proposition that an individual's place in the structure vitally affects how he is perceived, judged, treated, and reacted to. Similarly, a person's attitudes toward himself, others, the future, and the organization and its goals are all partly shaped by his locus in the system's subparts and roles. A structure like tracking, with its related social roles, labels, and identities, is both pervasive and visible. Thus, it should not be surprising if the critics are correct in contending that this subsystem itself influences the educational process and its outcome for students.

Despite the prevalence of tracking, there is little evidence on its educational effects. Such evidence as is available tends to support the critics. That students are often inaccurately assigned to tracks is illustrated by evidence presented in *Hobson v. Hansen* (1967, p. 490). On reevaluation by school psychologists, fully two-thirds of the students who were to be assigned to the lowest track in the District of Columbia schools in 1965 were considered to have been inaccurately evaluated. In fact, many were found to be capable of work at the level of the highest track. An earlier study in the Boston area reported:

. . . it is known, for example, that even very able boys from working class homes who fail to make really good grades in the seventh and eighth grades are seldom advised to take a college preparatory course. This is not equally true of boys from white collar homes (Stouffer, 1961, p. 176).

Some years earlier, a junior-high-school teacher described how the influence of family background operated in her school. Asked if there was "much class feeling" in her school, she responded:

Oh, yes, there is a lot of that. We try not to have it but of course we can't help it. Now, for instance, even in the sections we have, it is evident. Sections are supposed to be made up just on the basis of records in the school but it isn't and everybody knows it isn't. I know right in my own A section I have children who ought to be in the B section, but they are little socialites and so they stay in A. I didn't say there are children in B who should be in A but in the A section there are some who shouldn't be there. We have discussed it in faculty meetings but nothing is ever done. . . . (Warner, Havighurst, and Loeb, 1944, p. 174).

The scant evidence available on the movement of students between tracks also supports the position of the critics.[9]

The only large-scale study of the effects of the presence or absence of track systems, the Coleman report (Coleman *et al.*, 1966), revealed that there were no effects (Dyer, 1968). Because of sampling problems and unknown variations in curriculum organization in schools of both categories, any conclusions from that study must be cautiously drawn. A more fruitful approach would be a within-school analysis of the educational outcomes for students on different tracks who are equated on as many individual-level variables as possible.

As noted earlier, tracking is one form of ability grouping. The many studies on the educational effects of ability grouping at the elementary level have shown mixed or inconclusive results.[10] Some studies have shown positive effects of ability grouping as compared with heterogeneous grouping; others, negative effects; and still others, no effects. Tracking, however, differs from ability grouping per se in two vital ways: tracked students are homogeneously grouped across

[9]See Thelen (1967, pp. 30–31), Douglas (1964), Turner (1960), and *Hobson v. Hansen* (1967, pp. 459–463).

[10]For a summary of these studies, see Goldberg, Passow, and Justman (1966). See also Thelen (1967), Shores (1964), Borg (1966), Tillman and Hull (1964), and Westby-Gibson (1966).

classes *and* across grade levels. Therefore, any effects of ability grouping are likely to be cumulative and magnified in career-long track systems.

The evidence most directly applicable to the present study comes, not from schools in the United States, but from investigations in English schools of streaming, a practice similar to the track system. Elder (1965) has provided a useful summary of many of these studies.[11] The pattern is clear: lower-stream students evidence more negative self-images, lower academic achievement, greater academic deterioration, a higher dropout rate, and lower occupational aspirations. Elder contends that these differences partly result from the streaming system itself.

A comprehensive and penetrating study of one modern secondary school in England lends further credence to many of the criticisms of tracking (Hargreaves, 1967). At "Lumley," a boys' school, each student was assigned to one of five streams on the basis of ability and achievement, his score on the "11 plus" examination playing the major role in determining assignment. Students in the different streams were publicly recognized as high or low in status and were fairly segregated into different classes during most of the school day.

Hargreaves' findings clearly suggest that the streaming system magnifies the tendency of those assigned to the lower streams to be lower in commitment to and satisfaction with school. Specifically, lower-stream students were absent more often, had more negative attitudes toward school, engaged in more misconduct and delinquency, and attained lower levels of achievement. As we will see later in more detail, Hargreaves shows that these differences result from an interwoven web of stream-related influences: differential teacher expectations, stigma, the convergence of lower-stream students into a "delinquescent" subculture, declining self-esteem, and feelings of alienation.

Because the basic organization of streaming is very similar to that of tracking, Hargreaves' findings inevitably lead to the suspicion that the same psychological and interpersonal processes and the same educational outcomes characterize the track system in the United States. In fact, the negative effects of tracking on non-college-bound students may be even stronger in this country, since the Lumley streaming system was more open and flexible, permitting greater

[11]Among the studies Elder reviewed, two are especially relevant to this investigation: Douglas (1964) and Jackson (1964).

mobility between streams, than appears to be true of United States schools.

A landmark study of an American high school has also reported a relationship between track position and rebellion (Stinchcombe, 1964). Students in the college-prep track skipped school less often and were sent out of class for misbehaving less frequently than vocational students. The difference was especially marked for middle-class students, both male and female.

Two studies of high-school boys in the state of Oregon show that plans to attend or not to attend college are related to a number of outcome variables in a direction consistent with the critics. One of the studies found that non-college-bound students were more often delinquent and, once delinquent, were more often repeaters than were college-bound students (Frease, 1969). The non-college-bound were also lower in academic achievement and more negative in their attitudes toward school. The other study found that non-college-bound students had lower educational aspirations and expectations, lower levels of school involvement and performance, lower evaluations of their abilities, greater involvement in extraschool activities, and higher rates of dropout, misbehavior in school, and delinquency (Kelly, 1970). Both studies conclude that the system of stratification within the school whereby college-bound and non-college-bound students are differentiated either informally by friendship groups or formally by the track system partly accounts for these differences in educational and behavioral outcomes. The studies did not employ track position per se as the independent variable, since the sample was drawn from a number of different high schools with different kinds of curricular arrangements. Nevertheless, the findings suggest that the same processes described by Hargreaves may well be operative in the United States track system. At the very least, the evidence points to the need to study the outcomes of track position more carefully.

A Summary and a Preview

The theme of this chapter has been that the schools are falling short of their mission and that the causes may well lie within their own curricular and organizational processes. Specifically, it has been suggested that the track system, employed by about half the high schools in this country, may inadvertently contribute to many of the very problems the schools are seeking to avert: unequal opportunity, untapped potential, lack of interest in learning, and alienation and deviancy.

The track system emerged as a response to the greater diversity of students which accompanied compulsory education and the rapid decline in available work roles for adolescents. After a review of the educational rationales for the track system, a number of criticisms leveled at tracking were discussed. These arguments suggest that the shortcomings in educational outcomes may be traced in part to the track system itself. Finally, the chapter summarized various studies of ability grouping, streaming, and tracking which, viewed together, suggest that while the critics may be correct, further research is needed. If the present study helps fill this need even to a limited degree and if it stimulates further research by identifying key variables and processes, it will have been successful.

The remainder of the book, then, is devoted to a study of some of the effects of track position on student careers. The dependent or effect variables are over-all academic achievement, academic change during the high-school career, participation in extracurricular activities, misconduct in school, dropping out of school, and delinquency. Chapter 2 contains a brief description of the sample, research design, and methods of analysis. In Chapter 3 the results are presented and discussed, while in Chapter 4 several processes are suggested which, in combination, provide an explanation, or interpretation, of the findings. Chapter 5 discusses the educational implications of the study. In this concluding chapter, particular attention is focused on the need to develop and test entirely new and different learning-living-teaching environments, and several guidelines for such environments are offered.

CHAPTER 2

The Sample, Measurements, and Methods

During the summer of 1964, various data were collected from official school transcripts on the classes which had entered two Midwestern three-year high schools in September, 1961 (Schafer, 1965). At the time the data were collected, nearly all members of the sample had graduated, dropped out, or transferred to another school. We will call the two communities in which the schools were located "Industrial City" and "Academic Heights."

THE SCHOOLS AND THE STUDENTS

Industrial City High School

Industrial City High is located near the central business district of Industrial City, not far from the campus of a medium-sized state university. The economy of the community depends mainly on the automobile industry. The school building is a three-storied structure built several decades ago. Together with parking lots, the school occupies approximately two square blocks.

On the fourth Friday of September, 1963, the student body of Industrial City High totaled 1,272, distributed by grade as follows: 459 sophomores, 440 juniors, 353 seniors, and 20 special-education students.

Typically, the career of the incoming tenth-grader began the first morning of school in September at the sound of the 8:15 bell. His first experience was meeting his homeroom teacher and homeroom classmates, whom he would meet in this same fashion for the next three years. The following, drawn from the *Industrial City High School Handbook*, aptly describes the functions of the homeroom, which was heterogeneous in composition:

> Homerooms serve as administrative devices to help with such things as collection of book fees, reporting of attendance, supervision in the auditorium, and identification of students. This period is fifteen minutes long. Students are expected to come to homeroom with work to do.

Beginning at 8:30 and continuing throughout the day at 55-minute intervals (with 1 hour off for lunch), the students attended classes. While English, mathematics, and science classes were attended separately by "college-preparatory" and "general" students, other classes were attended jointly.

The professional staff of Industrial City High was distributed among the positions of principal, assistant principal, counselor, department chairman (who also taught), full-time teacher, and psychologist.

The principal's responsibility was to manage and direct the entire school program. His activities were divided between external and internal affairs, with the heaviest emphasis on internal coordination and planning of curricular and personnel matters. He also spent considerable time dealing with serious student-discipline problems. The months during which the data were gathered marked the end of the first academic year for this principal. A middle-aged former superintendent of a small school district, he succeeded a long-time principal who had begun his tenure prior to World War II and who therefore had seen the community and school undergo marked growth and compositional changes.

The assistant principal, who had occupied that position since the ninth grade shifted to the two new junior high schools in 1959, was concerned primarily, though not exclusively, with disciplining students for violations of school regulations regarding attendance, tardiness, dress, leaving the building during the school day without permission, and classroom and hall misconduct. He also shared in the management of other internal affairs of the school.

The three counselors were engaged mainly in administrative work centering around the enrollment, classification, and scheduling of students. In addition, they occasionally counseled students who had "emotional problems" or academic difficulties, who requested curriculum information, or who wished to apply for college entrance. These encounters with students, however, were secondary to work of a more clerical nature. There was a long-standing policy against any involvement of counselors in disciplining students.

The special-services staff, though housed in the building, was isolated from the affairs of the high school, serving the rest of the school system only. This department consisted of several diagnosticians, psychologists, and social workers. Though it had been in existence for several years during the former principal's tenure, it had been unable to win his favor, despite the intense interest of the special-services head as well as of his staff in serving high-school students. After gaining some acceptance by the new principal, this department became involved in dealing with "problem students" during the year of this research to the extent that one diagnostician (who also was head of the special-education department) received occasional referrals of such students for special counseling or testing.

Academic Heights High School

Academic Heights High is housed in a once spacious but now overcrowded multimillion-dollar complex, completed in 1956 and located near the edge of the city on a 177-acre campus that includes athletic fields, parking lots, and a forested area. The physical plant contains many progressive and unusual features: planetarium, weather station, and radio and television studios, among others. The school is located in the community of Academic Heights, a rapidly expanding city whose economy is based mainly on a large state university situated near the center of the city.

In comparison to the 1,272 students enrolled at Industrial City High in September, 1963, there were 2,641 students enrolled at Academic Heights High at that time. They were distributed by grade as follows: 893 sophomores, 949 juniors, 726 seniors, and 73 postgraduate and special-education students.

The daily routine for Academic Heights students began at 8:25 with first-hour classes. Periods were 55 minutes long, interrupted in the middle of the day by a 30-minute lunch and homeroom session.

As at Industrial City High, each student was assigned to a heterogeneous homeroom, the membership of which remained the same throughout the high-school career. It consisted of from 30 to 35 boys and girls supervised by a teacher who served during that period of the day as a "homeroom counselor." The homeroom performed several functions in addition to the purely administrative ones served by the Industrial City homeroom. Here, for instance, it served as the smallest unit of student government, as a base for social activities after school, and as a "breather" unit in the middle of the day. When official student-government or other administrative business did not occupy the period, it was taken up either by study or by conversation among the students. The homeroom counselors were an important link between the administration and the students, carrying on such activities as scheduling students' classes for upcoming semesters.

The professional staff of Academic Heights High was divided among the following positions: principal, assistant principal, counselor, social worker, college consultant, vocational coordinator, department chairman (who also taught), teacher (who usually was a homeroom counselor), comptroller, nurse, psychologist (part-time), and speech therapist (part-time).

Various occupants of these positions also sat on one or more of the following committees: (1) faculty committee, whose tasks were "to act in an advisory capacity to the Principal, to suggest recommendations in the areas of guidance and administration for consideration by the faculty, and to consider such problems of the school as may be suggested by the Principal or other members of the faculty"; (2) guidance committee, whose functions were "to study, evaluate, and plan the total guidance program, to serve as a clearing house for information concerning current developments in guidance, and to deal with adjustment problems of students" (most guidance-committee meetings attended by the senior author were taken up with discussion about and decisions on students who were in difficulty and whose cases a counselor or the assistant principal was hesitant to act on alone for one reason or another); (3) curriculum committee, whose major activities centered around modifying the curriculum and maintaining uniformity in instructional and evaluation practices.

The principal, who had occupied the position for more than two decades, spent most of his time on external matters (dealing in various ways with the central administration and with professional and community groups) and on higher-level administrative and policy matters within the school. By and large, he was directly involved only to a slight extent with student affairs, except for official matters such as school assemblies, important student-council meetings, and the like. Such involvement as did occur had to do mainly with students at the upper, rather than the lower, level of the status system. In contrast with the Industrial City principal, his time was only infrequently spent on disciplining or otherwise coping with deviant pupils.

Student discipline was the major concern of the Academic Heights assistant principal. His task was disciplining students for truancy, serious classroom disruption, smoking, theft, destruction of school property, fighting, and so on. He usually received referrals of students either from counselors, who handled less serious behavior problems, or directly from classroom teachers when, in their judgment, the seriousness of a deviant action warranted his attention.

The assistant principal constantly seemed overloaded with disciplinary cases and, as a consequence, spread himself more thinly across his other activities, which consisted of room scheduling, advising the student council, coordinating the testing program, supervising the attendance office, and assisting the principal in various other administrative details.

The daily routine of the 9 counselors (3 per grade level) contrasted considerably with that of the Industrial City counselors. Whereas the latters' duties consisted almost entirely of classifying students and scheduling their academic programs, much of the time detached from the students themselves, Academic Heights counselors spent more of their day meeting with students. For the most part these encounters were for the purpose of checking on unexcused absences, responding to teachers' complaints about the behavior or "attitude" of students, or counseling on academic matters such as course schedule or low grades. Most of the time was spent with a small percentage of students who, for one reason or another, deviated from expected patterns of student behavior. The remaining time was spent either in college counseling, in advising and coordinating student extracurricular activities, or in committee meetings.

The Academic Heights counselors frequently voiced to the senior author their dissatisfaction over the volume of paper work with which they saw themselves burdened and which prevented them from carrying out what they regarded as their proper function, academic and career counseling. Some counselors also spoke of the conflict which they experienced over the necessity to fulfill simultaneously the roles of counselor and minor disciplinarian. They reported finding it difficult to develop proper rapport with the students when their image was less counselor and more disciplinarian.

At Academic Heights High, teachers, counselors, and the assistant principal often saw students' academic or behavioral difficulties as rooted in emotional problems of one sort or another. In the case of such judgments, students often were referred to one of the two social workers (one of each sex), whose time was almost completely devoted to working with such pupils either on a long-term basis or on a crisis (emergency) basis. In addition to working directly with pupils, they also spent some time consulting with teachers, counselors, or the assistant principal about particular students or about more general matters, such as classroom sanctioning techniques. The boys' social worker carried on a group service program in which two groups of boys met once a week (during school hours), sometimes inside the building and other times elsewhere in the community. Programed activities, along with controlled group influence, were directed toward the alleviation of the members' academic and/or behavioral problems.[1]

The Schools and the Communities Contrasted

Whereas there were only two tracks for Industrial City students, Academic Heights High School had a four-track program. These tracks were listed in the *1961 Curriculum Guide* as Special Room, for those students who were mentally handicapped or retarded; General, Business, and Industrial Curricula, for those who planned to complete their formal education with a diploma from high school; College Curricula and University Curricula, for those who planned to attend a college or university; and Advanced Placement Program, for students with exceptionally high academic aptitude and superior achievement in specific subject-matter fields.

The *Curriculum Guide* stated that the four-track system was provided for two general purposes: first, to meet more adequately the wide range of individual differences, varying needs, and differing interests among its students; and second, to retain students in high school as long as they could profit from the experience. More specific objectives underlay the various tracks. For example, one of the objectives of the Special Room was to find full-time employment for students, even before the completion of three years in the high school. By comparison, one of the objectives of the Advanced Placement Program was to enable students to pass the national advanced-placement examination in order to gain advanced placement and credit toward their degrees from colleges or universities.

Three considerations were stressed as most important in the assignment of students to tracks: genuine interest, good habits of work, and proved aptitudes. These were considered most reliably indicated by the student's scholarship record, habits of study, preference for certain subjects, hobbies, and tested aptitudes and abilities.

For most purposes, these tracks could be collapsed into the two inclusive ones of college-preparatory and non-college-preparatory. Informal prestige was assigned by students, staff, and community in this way. Similarly, the "core" courses—English, social studies, mathe-

[1]For reports on this program, see Vinter and Sarri (1965) and Sarri and Vinter (1969).

matics, and science—were designated either by a "c" (college) or "g" (general, which included all non-college-preparatory curricula). For these reasons, our later analysis will be based on this dichotomous break.

There were several notable differences between the teaching staffs of the two high schools. First, the Academic Heights High teachers outnumbered the Industrial City High teachers by more than 2 to 1 (120 versus 55), reflecting the difference in student enrollment mentioned earlier. Second, a higher proportion of the Academic Heights were men (59 versus 51 per cent). Third, although the two teaching staffs did not differ in amount of total teaching experience (the median for both schools was 9 years), the average local tenure of the Academic Heights staff was somewhat shorter than that of the Industrial City staff. This differential was reflected in differences in median years taught at these particular schools (4 years versus 5 years) and in proportions who had taught there 4 years or less (52 versus 44 per cent) and 10 years or more (21 versus 33 per cent). Fourth, a higher proportion of Academic Heights teachers than Industrial City teachers reported in a questionnaire that they taught mostly college-preparatory courses (55 versus 34 per cent). This difference reflected similar differences in curriculum distribution of students by track, as will be shown later.

Selected demographic characteristics of Industrial City and Academic Heights are presented in Table 1. Comparison of the figures for the two communities reveals that Academic Heights is more than three times larger than Industrial City, contains a considerably smaller proportion of blacks, and is higher in levels of education and

TABLE 1. SELECTED DEMOGRAPHIC CHARACTERISTICS OF THE COMMUNITIES

	Industrial City	*Academic Heights*
Total population	20,957	67,340
White, %	77	94
Black, %	23	6
Median school years completed	11.4	14.3
High school, %	46	70
College, %	13	39
Median family income	\$6,956	\$7,550

Source: United States Bureau of the Census, *U.S. Census of Population: 1960*, Vol. 1: *Characteristics of the Population*, Part 24.

income. These community-wide socioeconomic differences are reflected in similar differences between the student bodies of the two schools, as shown below.

The figures in Table 2 indicate the distribution of students in each

TABLE 2. DISTRIBUTION BY FATHER'S OCCUPATION, RACE, AND MEASURED INTELLIGENCE, %

	Industrial City	*Academic Heights*
Father's occupation[a]		
Upper white-collar	18	49
Lower white-collar	10	13
Upper blue-collar	22	19
Lower blue-collar	37	15
Farm	5	1
Unknown	9	2
Race		
White	77	92
Black	23	6
Measured intelligence[b]		
120 or higher	20	24
110 or higher	46	47
100 or higher	69	71
90 or higher	85	87
80 or higher	95	95

[a] These labels are based on census categories.
[b] Industrial City scores are based on the Lorge-Thorndike Intelligence Test, taken during the ninth grade. Academic Heights scores are based on the California Test of Mental Maturity, taken during the tenth grade.

school by father's occupation, race, and measured intelligence. It is apparent that Industrial City High had a higher proportion of students from black families and blue-collar backgrounds. However, there is little difference in the distribution of intelligence-test scores, except at the highest levels. In both schools, the median and mean score is 108.

Despite the differences in racial and socioeconomic backgrounds between the schools, earlier analysis revealed virtually identical findings, not only in the apparent effects of track position, but also when several other factors were related to one another (Schafer, 1965). Therefore, it seems entirely justified to combine the two into a single sample. While the psychological, interpersonal, and organizational dynamics behind the findings may differ by school, the outcomes of track position are virtually identical.

For participation in extracurricular activities, only the students from Academic Heights were used, since comparable data were not available for the other school. The only instance when an entirely different sample was used was for the analysis of misconduct in school. Here the data consisted of referrals to the vice principal from all three classes enrolled in Academic Heights High during the 1963–1964 academic year.

THE MEASUREMENT OF SIX EDUCATIONAL OUTCOMES

We noted in Chapter 1 that the track to which a student is assigned represents a social position or category carrying status and value connotations. Many critics contend that for a variety of reasons, assignment to the college-preparatory track results in educational, social, and personal advantages, while assignment to a non-college-preparatory track constitutes serious disadvantages for educational and life chances, as well as for personal development. In research terms, then, track position will be treated as the independent or causal variable.

Track position is indicated by whether the student took English in the "college-prep" or the "general" section during the first semester of the tenth grade. (These were the transcript designations actually used in both schools.) If a student was in the college-prep section, he almost invariably had college-prep classes in other courses or he took courses such as advanced mathematics or a foreign language in which nearly all enrollees also were college-bound. As we will see in the next chapter, only a small proportion moved up or down in track after the first semester of the sophomore year. Table 3 reveals that at Academic Heights, 71 per cent of the student body were enrolled in the college-prep track, as compared with 58 per cent at Industrial City.

At Academic Heights High, students in three closely related cur-

TABLE 3. DISTRIBUTION BETWEEN TRACKS, %

	Industrial City	*Academic Heights*
College-prep	58	71
Non-college-prep	42	29
Total	100	100
N	(404)	(753)

ricula—University, College, and Advanced Placement—were designated in this study as college-prep. Students in the General, Retailing, Stenographic, General Office, Industrial, and Special Room curricula were designated as non-college-prep. Industrial City High had only two tracks, College-Prep and General.

The first dependent or effect variable, academic achievement, was indicated by each student's grade-point average (GPA) for all major courses for the tenth through the twelfth grade, as computed from grades recorded on the official transcript. Letter grades were transformed into numerical scores in such a way that an all-A average equaled 4.00, while all-E's average 0.00. The GPA was based on six semesters for those who graduated and from one to five semesters for those who transferred or dropped out prior to graduation. GPA's were divided into quartiles within each school and then combined into a single sample.[2] Thus, each student's academic achievement was ranked relative to others with whom he had originally been compared by his teachers.

Academic change, the second dependent variable, was indicated by whether students moved up or down or remained stable between the first semester of high school and each subsequent semester. This analysis, based on separate GPA's for each term, is presented in the form of separate trends for college-prep and non-college-prep students. Eventual dropouts were excluded from these tables, since their low early achievement and subsequent departure would have artificially increased the over-all downward pattern between the sophomore year and later years.

Participation in extracurricular activities, the third dependent variable, was measured by the number of entries in the yearbook for the three years of high school. These data were available only at Academic Heights High. Students were grouped into three categories: no activities, one or two, and three or more.

The fourth dependent variable, misconduct in school, was indicated by whether or not the vice principal of Academic Heights High had recorded on disciplinary cards in his office the student's name and, if so, whether or not the student was then suspended from school. For all students enrolled during the 1963–1964 year, tabulations were made by track as to the number of students with one or more recorded violations, three or more recorded violations, and at least one suspension. These percentages were compared with the percentages in each track of the class which entered as tenth-graders in the fall of 1961.

[2]The cutoff points are presented on page 37.

The fifth dependent variable, dropping out, was established directly from each student's transcript. The semester of last attendance was recorded for each individual. Those who remained in school through the last semester of the senior year were designated as graduates, and the rest were designated as either transfers or dropouts. Those who were not enrolled by the end of the senior year and for whom a transcript had not been sent to another school, according to school records, were designated as dropouts.

The sixth dependent variable, delinquency, was indicated by whether a student in the sample of 1,157 had an official juvenile-court record, according to court files. It must be recognized that court records greatly underestimate rates of actual delinquency and may underestimate middle-class and therefore upper-track delinquency. The findings, then, must be viewed cautiously, especially if they yield lower rates for upper-track students.

All students with delinquent records were divided into two groups, those who had developed a record prior to the beginning of the second semester of their sophomore year and those whose first contact with the court had occurred after that point. This time line separated those students who first became officially delinquent after having been on their high-school track for at least one semester from those who had developed prior records—for whom track position could not yet have contributed to delinquency. The court data were collected in 1967, but only pregraduation offenses were coded for this study.

To investigate the independent effect of track position on these six educational outcomes, it is necessary to separate track position from other previous or extraneous influences. It is entirely possible, for example, that one might find a higher level of academic achievement for college-prep students but that this would be the result, not of track position, but of higher ability, motivation, or parental pressures to begin with. In other words, the finding might result from selection factors rather than from the influence of track position. Therefore, it is important somehow to control for or hold constant as many other influences as possible.

In reality, it is seldom possible to eliminate selection factors completely, especially in studies in natural settings. Nevertheless, it frequently is feasible to eliminate the effects of many extraneous influences, thereby increasing the likelihood that it is indeed the independent variable and not something else that is making the difference in outcomes. In this study, three controls were introduced at different points in the analysis: father's occupation, measured intelligence, and pre-high-school academic achievement. While these do not represent all possible selection differences between students on the two tracks, controlling for them provides for greater confidence that the findings were in fact the result of track position. At several points, the independent influence of these factors was also compared with the independent influence of track position.

Father's occupation, indicated from school records in Academic Heights High and from a brief questionnaire administered to graduating seniors in Industrial City High, was divided into white-collar and blue-collar. Measured intelligence (IQ) for Industrial City students was based on scores on the Lorge-Thorndike Intelligence Test and, for Academic Heights students, scores on the California Test of Mental Maturity as recorded in the students' official records. The scores for the two tests were treated as equivalent, inasmuch as the test means and standard deviations were identical for the national test samples.[3] The means also were identical for the two schools (108). This was the cutoff point for dividing all students into high and low categories. Previous achievement, also dichotomized, was measured by GPA for the final semester of junior high school, according to the transcript. Students whose 9B GPA was 2.50 or higher were categorized as high previous achievers, and the rest were considered low previous achievers.

The quantitative data presented above were supplemented by field notes collected by the senior author during several weeks of informal, exploratory visits to the two schools. During this period, he visited classes, committee meetings, and faculty meetings; talked informally with administrators, counselors, teachers, and students; conducted semistructured interviews; and observed behavior in and around school. Immediately after leaving the school building, he dictated impressions and notes for later typing. These relatively unstructured and unfocused observations and interviews turned out to be useful both for sharpening our focus on tracking as a key structural influence on behavior and, later, for interpreting the quantitative findings.

THE METHOD OF ANALYSIS

The method of analysis employed throughout the study was simple percentage differences. In most cases, zero-order tables (with controls) were followed by third-order tables in an effort to reexamine the relationship with selection factors controlled out. The procedure

[3]See *Examiner's Manual: California Short-Form Test of Mental Maturity* (1963) and *Examiner's Manual: The Lorge-Thorndike Intelligence Tests* (1957).

used to hold control variables constant was a weighted-percentage approach known as test-factor standardization (Anderson and Zelditch, 1968, pp. 175–178). In brief, test-factor standardization is analogous to partial correlation. With categorical or ordinal percentage data in tabular form, it allows the investigator to collapse a contingency table with several partials back into a single table without partials, by averaging the partials according to their size. This method has the advantage of permitting simple comparisons of percentages between zero-order and first-, second-, or third-order tables.

THE LIMITATIONS OF THE STUDY

This study must be viewed as suggestive, exploratory, and tentative, rather than definitive and conclusive. Despite the limitations inherent in the sample, design, and data, however, the findings should not be taken lightly, especially since they fall into a rather marked and consistent pattern. In educational and social-science research, modest studies which focus on key questions and produce clear and strong findings often have the greatest long-run impact on theory or policy. At the very least, they generate more complete and intensive investigations of the theoretical or policy issue.

One important limitation in this study is the sample, which consists of only 1,157 students attending only two schools in a particular region of the country during a particular period of time. Whether the findings would be the same with other students in other places at different times cannot be accurately known. The reader must exercise obvious caution, then, in drawing conclusive inferences from these data about schools generally or about any other particular school. On the other hand, there is little reason to suspect that these schools are especially unusual. Therefore, it does not seem unwarranted to *suggest* that the findings reported in the next chapter *might* characterize other schools and students. As we shall see, they certainly indictate the need for research on a larger, randomly selected sample.

Another limitation is the influence of uncontrolled extraneous or confounding variables. In other words, non-college-prep students may enter school with less motivation or ability, even though they are equal to college-prep students in (1) measured intelligence, (2) father's occupation, and (3) previous achievement. An important drawback of our method of data analysis which adds to this limitation is that the control variables are only dichotomized. Thus, a college-prep student matched with a non-college-prep student on the three control variables may be less likely to drop out, not only because his parents or peers pressure him to stay in school (influences for which we have no measures), but also because he may be higher *within* the upper category of these three control variables. Even so, the findings suggest that social-psychological factors associated with track position, rather than prior differences or uncontrolled simultaneous influences, account for differences between college-prep and non-college-prep students in over-all academic achievement, trends in achievement, participation in extracurricular activities, misconduct in school, dropping out, and delinquency.

A limitation confronting many behavioral-science studies, but largely avoided in this study, is the questionable validity of the measures. GPA, dropout, IQ, sex, and father's occupation were all recorded from official school transcripts. Participation in extracurricular activities was obtained from the yearbooks of Academic Heights High, while delinquency was recorded from juvenile-court records. The school data no doubt contained random errors of unknown numbers, stemming from mistakes by school officials in recording transcript and yearbook information and by the researchers in transferring the raw data onto code sheets. The court data must be viewed only as gross underapproximations of actual violations of the law, and may well underrepresent the delinquent behavior of college-prep students, who are disproportionately middle-class and are thus less likely to be entered on court records, even when detected by police. Nevertheless, all the data from the school and the court records correlated as expected with variables, as shown in the next chapter and in the Appendix. This test of "external validity" suggests, then, that the data indeed measured the variables intended.

Finally—and this is not so much a limitation of the quality of the design and data as it is of the scope of the study—the data consisted of measures only of the end variables (independent and dependent) and did not permit the determination of what psychological, interpersonal, or contextual factors intervened between track position and the educational and behavioral outcomes. Thus, we cannot answer the question "Why does track position make a difference?" but must limit ourselves simply to observing that it does. This finding is still a contribution to the state of knowledge. And, fortunately, we are able to draw on more general theory in sociology, social psychology, and education, as well as on other specific studies, to offer intelligent speculation about intervening processes.

CHAPTER 3

The Findings of the Study

The first part of this chapter is devoted to an analysis of the types of students assigned to the two tracks. This issue is vital, for an understanding not only of some of the determinants of this decision-point along the educational pathway, but also of what types of students are exposed to the different influences of the two tracks. In the remainder of the chapter, we report findings on the relationship between track position, on the one hand, and academic achievement, academic change, participation in extracurricular activities, misconduct in school, dropping out, and delinquency, on the other.

The Assignment to Tracks

The previous chapter reported that a majority of incoming sophomores were assigned to the college-prep track in both schools: 58 per cent at Industrial City and 71 per cent at Academic Heights. Just how students were assigned to—or chose—tracks remains something of a mystery. Interviews with teachers and counselors in both high schools and their feeder junior high schools indicated that assignment to the different tracks resulted from a combination of factors: student desires and aspirations, teacher advice, achievement-test scores, grades, pressure from parents, and counselor assessment of academic promise. In both communities, ninth-grade counselors reported that grades, achievement-test scores, and recommendations from English and math teachers weighed especially heavily in their decisions. If the track-assignment process at these schools operates like the one studied by Cicourel and Kitsuse (1963), the assumptions made by counselors about "character" and "adjustment" also probably played an important part, intentional or inadvertent, in the assignment of students.

Whatever the precise dynamics of the decisions, the outcome was clear in the schools we studied: coming from a white-collar family of the white race substantially increased a student's chances of entering the college-prep track. As shown in Table 4, 83 per cent of white-collar youth, compared with 48 per cent of those from blue-collar homes, enrolled in the college-prep track. The relationship with race is even stronger: 72 per cent of whites and 30 per cent of blacks were assigned to the college-prep track.

TABLE 4. DISTRIBUTION BETWEEN TRACKS BY FATHER'S OCCUPATION AND RACE, %

	College-Prep	*Non-College-Prep*	*Total*	*N*
Father's occupation[a]				
White-collar	83	17	100	(583)
Blue-collar	48	52	100	(518)
Race[b]				
White	72	28	100	(1,005)
Black	30	70	100	(139)

[a] No data were available for 56 cases.
[b] No data were available for 13 cases.

It is not surprising that IQ and previous achievement (last semester of junior high school) were also associated with track assignment, as shown in Table 5. The same table reveals that girls were only somewhat more likely than boys to be assigned to the college-prep track. Thus, sex was apparently not as important a factor in track assignment as were the other variables.

TABLE 5. DISTRIBUTION BETWEEN TRACKS BY IQ, PREVIOUS ACHIEVEMENT, AND SEX, %

	College-Prep	*Non-College-Prep*	*Total*	*N*
IQ[a]				
High	91	9	100	(549)
Low	45	55	100	(564)
Previous achievement[b]				
High	90	10	100	(530)
Low	44	56	100	(577)
Sex				
Boys	62	38	100	(595)
Girls	68	32	100	(562)

[a] No IQ test scores were available for 44 cases.
[b] No 9B GPA data were available for 50 cases.

Table 6 lends additional support for the assertion that race and socioeconomic background were important influences on track assignment. By utilizing the test-factor standardization method for controlling, we found that father's occupation and race continued to be associated with track assignment even after the effects of IQ and previous achievement were partialed out or eliminated.[1] Previous analysis revealed that the relationships held after reading-test scores were controlled as well (Schafer and Armer, 1966).[2]

TABLE 6. DISTRIBUTION BETWEEN TRACKS BY FATHER'S OCCUPATION AND RACE, STANDARDIZED FOR IQ AND PREVIOUS ACHIEVEMENT, %*

	College-Prep	*Non-College-Prep*	*Total*	*N*
Father's occupation				
White-collar	81	19	100	(569)
Blue-collar	50	50	100	(496)
Race				
White	69	30	99	(966)
Black	32	67	99	(132)

*This table is derived from Tables I and II in the Appendix.

We suggest the reader compare these findings with the high school's formally stated criteria for track assignment presented in Chapter 2. Without data on each incoming sophomore's college aspirations, it was impossible to claim direct discrimination by social class or race. Nevertheless, the observations of other writers suggest that teachers and counselors in these two schools may well have been influenced in subtle and unrecognized ways by inferences about students' backgrounds, based on style of dress, interpersonal demeanor, place of residence, or knowledge of the school performance of older brothers or sisters. Their direct knowledge of family background may have had a more recognized and intended effect, as Cicourel and Kitsuse (1963) suggest: given a limited capacity for college-prep students in the schools (as set by assignment of teachers

[1]The procedure involved in the computation of Table 6 and the following standardized tables was quite simple. First, the data were sorted, or controlled, on each variable; then percentages were computed for each resulting category. These percentages were then averaged according to the proportión of the total sample they represented, so that, in effect, we ended up with a table of weighted percentages. The same procedure was used to derive the weighted-mean-difference tables shown later, except that the differences in percentage between variable categories, rather than the actual percentages, were averaged according to the proportion of the sample they represented.

[2]Readers interested in greater statistical detail may consult the appropriate tables in the Appendix, as indicated in footnotes to the tables in the text.

and sectioning of classes), white-collar and white students may have been judged to be better success risks than were students from blue-collar and black families.

In any case, lower-income and minority-group students were disproportionately subject to whatever negative effects are associated with the non-college-prep track. As we will see shortly, these effects appear to have been substantial. Moreover, this track became the repository for students who not only had been less successful in school in the past, but also had been officially identified, via track assignment, as less capable and promising. Thus, the stage was set by the formal structure itself for the convergence of students with less than favorable self-images, attitudes, and norms. Subsequent experiences in school may well have intensified these attributes.

The track-assignment decision was almost irreversible, at least during high school. Only 7 per cent of those who began on the college-prep track shifted to the non-college-prep track, while only 7 per cent moved in the other direction. This fact strongly suggests that whatever educational deficiencies (at least as defined by the school) the non-college-prep students had at the time of their track assignment persisted, rather than were corrected, as a result of their assignment to that track. The theoretical justification or rationale for tracking—that low-achieving students, when separated into homogeneous groups, will receive better instruction which will prepare and enable them to switch to higher tracks—is not supported by the findings of this study. Neither is there support for the assumption that low-achievers will be provided maximum opportunities for transferring to higher tracks. Without this educational improvement and upgrading of low-track students, the track system, in a very real sense, can be viewed as a virtual caste system, with a high degree of closure and formal segregation. Greater mobility than was encountered in these schools has been reported in modern English secondary schools, despite the customary view that streaming is more rigid and fixed than tracking (Hargreaves, 1967). It must be borne in mind, though, that the more rigid separation in England is *between* the modern secondary school and the grammar school, and not within the former.

Studies of streaming in England (Hargreaves, 1967; Douglas, 1964; Jackson, 1964) and of friendship patterns among students with different college plans in the United States (Haller and Butterworth, 1960; McDill and Coleman, 1963, 1965; Alexander and Campbell, 1964; Campbell and Alexander, 1965) suggest that the formal separation of students by the track system probably gives rise to relatively distinct and separate informal friendship patterns as well. A growing polarization of these subgroupings into proschool and antischool positions has been suggested by several writers. The following examination of some of the apparent educational and social effects of track position suggests they may well be correct.

THE EFFECTS OF TRACK POSITION

Academic Achievement

Does track position independently affect grades? Although we cannot be entirely certain because of the simultaneous influence of other factors, the data strongly suggest that it does. Table 7 shows that a far greater percentage of college-prep than non-college-prep students placed in the high-GPA group of their class (37 versus 2 per cent), while more than four times as great a percentage of non-college-prep students fell in the low-achievement group (52 versus 11 per cent).

TABLE 7. DIFFERENCE BETWEEN TRACKS IN ACADEMIC ACHIEVEMENT, %*

	High	*High Average*	*Low Average*	*Low*	*Total*	*N*
College-prep	37	29	23	11	100	(752)
Non-college-prep	2	16	30	52	100	(405)

*The cutoff points for GPA are as follows:

	Industrial City	*Academic Heights*
High	2.59 and above	2.86 and above
High average	1.90–2.58	2.28–2.85
Low average	1.44–1.89	1.77–2.27
Low	1.43 and below	1.76 and below

Clearly, the difference in achievement is great. But to what extent is it caused by factors associated with track position itself, as against other factors? It is often argued, as an alternative explanation, that non-college-prep students do less well in schoolwork because of their family backgrounds. These students, it is said, more often come from lower-class homes, where grades and college are less highly valued, achievement is encouraged and rewarded less frequently, books and help in schoolwork are less available, and the language is of lower quality. Others would contend that the difference in academic achievement shown in Table 7 can be explained by the fact that college-prep students simply are brighter because of their heredity or more favorable environment or both; after all, this is one of the reasons they were selected for the college-prep track. Still others would argue that non-college-prep students earn lower grades because they performed less well in elementary school and junior high school, have fallen behind in the accumulation of learning, and probably try less hard in high school.

Probably, each of these alternative explanations is partly valid. No doubt it is true that non-college-prep students tend to receive lower grades in part because they more often come from lower-class families, have lower IQ scores, and have developed an accumulated deficit in learning through lower performance at earlier grade levels. Fortunately, it is possible with our data to separate the influence of track position from these other factors by controlling for father's occupation, IQ, and GPA for the last semester of junior high school.

Table 8 shows that even when the effects of these confounding factors are eliminated through test-factor standardization, there remains a sizable difference in GPA between tracks. For instance, an average of 35 per cent of non-college-prep students fell in the low-achievement group, compared with 12 per cent of those on the college-prep track. This pattern, similar for boys and girls (see Table IV in the Appendix), clearly suggests that assignment to the non-college-prep track has a rather strong negative influence on grades. While past performance, family background, and measured ability clearly affect achievement, we contend that it is simplistic to attribute track differences in grades entirely to these confounding or selection factors.

TABLE 8. DIFFERENCE BETWEEN TRACKS IN ACADEMIC ACHIEVEMENT, STANDARDIZED FOR FATHER'S OCCUPATION, IQ, AND PREVIOUS ACHIEVEMENT, %*

	High	*High Average*	*Low Average*	*Low*	*Total*	*N*
College-prep	30	31	27	12	100	(681)
Non-college-prep	4	23	38	35	100	(326)

*This table is derived from Table III in the Appendix.

It is significant that the independent effect of track position on GPA was greater for track position than for previous achievement, father's occupation, or IQ, when each of the others is held constant. This fact is revealed in Table 9, which presents the weighted mean dif-

TABLE 9. WEIGHTED MEAN DIFFERENCE IN ACADEMIC ACHIEVEMENT BY TRACK, PREVIOUS ACHIEVEMENT, FATHER'S OCCUPATION, AND IQ, %*

	Mean Difference in High Group	*Mean Difference in Low Group*
Track	31	32
Previous achievement	14	18
Father's occupation	12	9
IQ	11	9

*This table is derived from Table III in the Appendix.

ference between college-prep and non-college-prep students in the percentage achieving in the high group and in the low group of their class. When previous achievement, father's occupation, and IQ were controlled, for instance, a weighted-average percentage difference of 31 points still separated college-prep from non-college-prep students in achievement in the high group of the class, and 32 points separated students in the low group. In short, track position appears to exert not only a strong effect on achievement, but a stronger effect than variables shown in past research to be among the most powerful predictors of achievement.

Also significant is the fact that previous achievement had a relatively strong effect on high-school achievement, though not so great as track position. This finding, combined with the previously observed lack of transferring between tracks, lends strong support for the contention that previously accrued educational deficits of students are not remedied within the track system, that relative educational advantages and disadvantages which students have previously experienced are formally and informally reinforced rather than corrected by tracking.

Academic Change

We have seen that students' track position is related to their overall academic achievement; yet several important questions remain. Were there changes in students' academic achievement during their high-school careers? In what direction(s) did their achievement change? And most important, did students' track position have any effect on changes in achievement? These questions are particularly important since the rationale for tracking is based in large part on the assumption that all students, fast learners and slow learners, educationally advantaged and disadvantaged, will benefit academically when separated into tracks. If this premise is indeed true, students in both college-prep and non-college-prep tracks should tend equally to experience academic improvement during their high-school careers.

Table 10 shows a marked tendency for academic improvement between the first and last semesters of high school.[3] In the highest beginning category (3.0 and above), a far higher percentage re-

TABLE 10. DISTRIBUTION ON ACADEMIC CHANGE, %*

10A GPA	*Up*	*Stable*	*Down*	*Total*	*N*
3.0 and above	0	83	17	100	(193)
2.5–2.9	49	27	24	100	(148)
2.0–2.4	52	24	24	100	(203)
1.5–1.9	68	19	13	100	(171)
1.4 and below	80	20	0	100	(153)

*This table includes only students who graduated and is based on a comparison of grades earned in semesters 10A and 12B.

mained stable than declined, while in the lowest beginning category (1.4 and below), a higher percentage improved than remained stable. In the middle categories, a markedly higher percentage improved than declined.

It is clear that, in general, academic achievement tended to improve. But what effect did track position have on academic change? A detailed answer to this question is provided in Table 11, which shows change between the beginning semester and each subsequent semester by track. Among college-prep students who began with a GPA of 1.4 or below, for example, a consistently and increasingly greater percentage improved each semester than remained stable. On the other hand, a notably smaller percentage of non-college-prep students in the same beginning category improved. The same tendency can be seen for students who began with GPA's between 2.5 and 2.9. Between semester 10A and 12B, for instance, 50 per cent of the non-college-prep students, compared to only 19 per cent of the college-prep students, declined in academic achievement. Although the percentages for non-college-prep students were based on rather small N's, the tendency for more non-college-prep than college-prep stu-

[3]As noted in Chapter 2, students who dropped out prior to graduation were not included in the analysis of academic change. Students were placed in the "up" or "down" category when they moved up or down at least one of the GPA categories in the table.

TABLE 11. DIFFERENCE BETWEEN TRACKS IN ACADEMIC CHANGE FROM BEGINNING SEMESTER TO EACH SUBSEQUENT SEMESTER, %

10A GPA	*College-Prep*				*Non-College-Prep*			
	Up	*Stable*	*Down*	*N*	*Up*	*Stable*	*Down*	*N*
3.0 and above								
10A to 10B	—	87	13	(206)	(1)	(2)	(6)	(9)
10A to 11A	—	78	22	(193)	(1)	(0)	(8)	(9)
10A to 11B	—	81	19	(191)	(1)	(2)	(6)	(9)
10A to 12A	—	89	11	(185)	(1)	(4)	(4)	(9)
10A to 12B	—	84	16	(184)	(1)	(4)	(4)	(9)
2.5–2.9								
10A to 10B	14	61	25	(134)	4	60	36	(25)
10A to 11A	39	31	30	(127)	4	33	63	(24)
10A to 11B	33	33	34	(124)	12	25	63	(24)
10A to 12A	47	33	20	(124)	17	38	45	(24)
10A to 12B	54	27	19	(124)	21	29	50	(24)
2.0–2.4								
10A to 10B	32	42	26	(150)	19	51	30	(71)
10A to 11A	37	33	30	(144)	13	33	54	(67)
10A to 11B	37	34	29	(142)	13	38	49	(63)
10A to 12A	54	28	18	(138)	28	41	31	(64)
10A to 12B	55	23	22	(138)	42	34	23	(64)
1.5–1.9								
10A to 10B	66	25	9	(126)	16	55	29	(56)
10A to 11A	52	26	22	(120)	34	32	34	(53)
10A to 11B	57	30	13	(119)	38	32	30	(53)
10A to 12A	75	15	10	(114)	50	25	25	(52)
10A to 12B	78	14	8	(118)	47	28	25	(53)
1.4 and below								
10A to 10B	63	37	—	(115)	35	65	—	(66)
10A to 11A	68	32	—	(106)	21	79	—	(62)
10A to 11B	71	29	—	(104)	50	50	—	(60)
10A to 12A	84	16	—	(98)	63	37	—	(57)
10A to 12B	92	8	—	(98)	60	40	—	(53)

dents' grades to decline in each comparison was consistent among all students whose beginning GPA's ranged from 2.5 to 1.5. On the other hand, a greater percentage of college-prep than non-college-prep students' grades improved in each semester comparison within that range of beginning grades. In short, the tendency for academic improvement was much stronger among college-prep students than among non-college-prep students, while decline in academic achievement more often occurred among non-college-prep students.

Extracurricular Participation

Assignment to a particular track is likely to have effects that are not singular and isolated. Rather, these effects are woven together into a complex pattern of attitudes, behavior, and performance in school, relations with other students and teachers, and even out-of-school behavior. Several writers have observed that within the school, non-college-prep students are more likely to be outside the mainstream of student life, partly because they feel marginal and put down and partly because by this time they have developed friendships with others who feel equally marginal and whose social life and interests revolve about other places and activities.

The figures in Table 12 show rates of participation in extracurricular activities during the three years of high school by track for

TABLE 12. DIFFERENCE BETWEEN TRACKS IN EXTRACURRICULAR PARTICIPATION, %

	Three or More Activities	*One or Two Activities*	*No Activities*	*Total*	*N*
College-prep	44	35	21	100	(537)
Non-college-prep	11	31	58	100	(216)

Academic Heights students. A marked difference in participation is evident by track. For instance, 44 per cent of college-prep students participated in three or more activities during high school, compared with only 11 per cent of non-college-prep students. Table 13 reveals

TABLE 13. DIFFERENCE BETWEEN TRACKS IN EXTRACURRICULAR PARTICIPATION, STANDARDIZED FOR FATHER'S OCCUPATION, IQ, AND PREVIOUS ACHIEVEMENT, %*

	Three or More Activities	*One or Two Activities*	*No Activities*	*Total*	*N*
College-prep	41	35	24	100	(512)
Non-college-prep	15	35	50	100	(199)

*This table is derived from Table V in the Appendix.

that a sizable difference remained even when father's occupation, IQ, and previous achievement were held constant, while Table 14 shows that track position related more strongly than any of these other fac-

TABLE 14. WEIGHTED MEAN DIFFERENCE IN EXTRACURRICULAR PARTICIPATION BY TRACK, PREVIOUS ACHIEVEMENT, FATHER'S OCCUPATION, AND IQ, %*

	Mean Difference
Track	27
Previous achievement	22
Father's occupation	19
IQ	13

*This table is based on the following categories of participation: one or more activities and no activities. The table is derived from Table V in the Appendix.

tors to participation. This relationship held for both boys and girls (see Table VI in the Appendix).

The negative effects of this social marginality for non-college-prep students are likely to be both short-term and long-run. In the short run, nonparticipation probably results in progressively greater alienation from school, since the non-college-bound are not only on the bottom, looking up academically, but also on the outside, looking in socially. Moreover, there is the loss of potential positive educational influences from college-bound students and from the teachers who sponsor activities (who probably have a greater effect than do teachers who do not sponsor activities because of the close relationships they are likely to develop with students). As a result, many marginal students probably turn even further away from school in search for substitute sources of fun and meaning. Our findings related to misconduct in school, dropout rates, and delinquency lend considerable credence to this argument.

In the long run, participants in extracurricular activities benefit from practice in performing social roles, setting up and maintaining social organizations, and contributing to some common goal. Such skills often are invaluable for securing white-collar employment and for subsequent occupational success. Moreover, studies have shown that participants in both service and athletic activities are more likely to aspire to college, because of positive peer influences, encouragement from teachers and counselors, and other reasons (Schafer and Armer, 1968; Rehberg and Schafer, 1968; Spady, 1970; Snyder, 1969). Track position and extracurricular participation may well be intervening influences, then, between social background and educational and social attainment.

Misconduct in School

Every principal is confronted with continual pressures to maintain order in his school. These pressures come from outside the school (adults expect teenagers to be kept off the streets during the day and to obey school authorities while in attendance), as well as from inside (teachers expect the bureaucracy to run reasonably quietly and on schedule so that they can get on with the job of teaching—and instilling respect for authority—and so that they will not be unduly threatened by their students). The sheer size of most schools makes the management of masses of students difficult enough, but the fact that many students are in school only because they must, by law, further exacerbates the task.

When a student misbehaves and violates school rules, most teachers and principals blame his parents, bad influences from his friends, or his own personality defects. But the data in Table 15 suggest that rebellion and misbehavior may be partly caused

TABLE 15. DISTRIBUTION BETWEEN TRACKS ON MISCONDUCT IN SCHOOL, %*

	College-Prep	*Non-College-Prep*	*Unknown*	*Total*	*N*
One or more violations	36	53	11	100	(220)
Three or more violations	19	70	11	100	(37)
Suspension	37	51	12	100	(65)
Percentage of all students in each track[a]	71	29	0	100	(753)

*The data on misconduct were based on violations recorded in the vice principal's office for students from all three classes during the 1963–1964 year at Academic Heights High.

[a]These data were only for the students who entered Academic Heights High as sophomores in the fall of 1961, most of whom were seniors during the year when the misconduct data were collected. There is no reason to believe this class differed from others in distribution between tracks.

by the school system itself, through its track system. Utilizing discipline records kept by the vice principal of Academic Heights High, we recorded information on types of offenses, disciplinary action taken, and track position of offenders during the 1963–1964 year. (These misconduct data, then, were based on deviants from all three grades, not just from the graduating class of 1964.)

Table 15 reveals that whereas non-college-prep students made up 29 per cent of the graduating class of 1964, they comprised 53 per cent of all students from the school who had misbehaved with sufficient seriousness to have been sent to the vice principal at least once, 70 per cent of those with three or more recorded violations, and 51 per cent of those who were suspended.

The data do not establish a definite causal linkage between track position and misconduct, especially since selection variables were unavailable. But they do lend tentative support to the suggestion that something happens to, between, and within non-college-prep students once they have been assigned to that track that leads to resentment, declining commitment to school, and rebellion. If large size and compulsory attendance make the job of behavior management difficult, the track system appears to make the task even more formidable. Our findings on dropout rates lend still further support to this position.

Dropout Rate

Does track position also influence the chance that students will graduate or drop out? Table 16 indicates that the chances of

TABLE 16. DIFFERENCE BETWEEN TRACKS IN DROPOUT RATE, %

	Graduated	*Transferred*	*Dropped Out*	*Total*	*N*
College-prep	86	10	4	100	(752)
Non-college-prep	57	7	36	100	(405)

dropping out were nine times greater if the student was on the non-college-prep track (36 versus 4 per cent). Again, it is possible that it was not track position itself that exerted this negative effect on the non-college-bound, but rather that the percentage difference resulted from differences in educational ability, aspiration, or commitment which students brought with them at the beginning of high school or from the simultaneous influence of other factors related to peers, family, or self.

In order to reduce the influence of extraneous or simultaneous factors, it was useful to separate track position from father's occupation, measured intelligence, and previous achievement. Table 17 shows that, on the average, non-college-prep students

TABLE 17. DIFFERENCE BETWEEN TRACKS IN DROPOUT RATE, STANDARDIZED FOR FATHER'S OCCUPATION, IQ, AND PREVIOUS ACHIEVEMENT, %*

	Graduated	*Transferred*	*Dropped Out*	*Total*	*N*
College-prep	88	8	4	100	(681)
Non-college-prep	74	7	19	100	(326)

*This table is derived from Table VII in the Appendix.

still dropped out in considerably greater numbers than did college-prep students (19 versus 4 per cent). As before, the relationship held among boys and girls alike (see Table VIII in the Appendix).

The findings shown in Table 18 reveal that track position made little difference in dropout rate among students who were aver-

TABLE 18. DIFFERENCES BETWEEN TRACKS IN DROPOUT RATE, CONTROLLING FOR ACADEMIC ACHIEVEMENT, %

	Graduated	*Transferred*	*Dropped Out*	*Total*	*N*
High					
College-prep	89	10	1	100	(278)
Non-college-prep	(5)	(1)	(1)	100	(7)
High average					
College-prep	88	9	3	100	(218)
Non-college-prep	87	8	5	100	(65)
Low average					
College-prep	84	12	4	100	(174)
Non-college-prep	72	8	20	100	(121)
Low					
College-prep	66	15	19	100	(82)
Non-college-prep	37	6	57	100	(212)

age-achievers or high-achievers in high school. However, it made a great deal of difference among low-achievers. For instance, 57 per cent of non-college-prep students who achieved in the low group of their class dropped out, compared with 19 per cent of low-achieving college-prep students. Viewed differently, a student's chances of dropping out if he fell in the low group of his class in achievement was about three times greater if he was a non-college-prep student than if he were a college-prep student. Although the percentage of students in both tracks who dropped out increased in each low-achievement group, the comparable percentages were greater among non-college-prep students. As a minimal interpretation, low achievement on the college-prep track seemed to be accompanied with more positive educational and social support, probably from classmates and teachers as well as parents, to effect continuation in school.

Table 19 reveals that track position independently related to dropout rate more strongly than did previous achievement, father's

TABLE 19. WEIGHTED MEAN DIFFERENCE IN DROPOUT RATE BY TRACK, PREVIOUS ACHIEVEMENT, IQ, AND FATHER'S OCCUPATION, %*

	Mean Difference
Track	18
Previous achievement	11
IQ	8
Father's occupation	5

*This table is derived from Table VII in the Appendix.

occupation, or IQ. These findings, along with others already reported, suggest that the non-college-prep experience has a dampening effect on commitment to school and that it independently contributes to resentment, frustration, and hostility, finally ending for many youth in active withdrawal from the alienating situation of school.

Delinquency Rate

As a principal agency of socialization, the high school seeks to foster a commitment to law-abiding behavior among teenagers. Among the vast majority of youth, the school has been fairly successful, at least until the era of widespread drug use. But if non-college-prep track position generates a sense of stigma, frustration, and marginality resulting in higher rates of misconduct in school and in a higher dropout rate, might it not also contribute to delinquency outside the school?

The figures in the top part of Table 20 indicate that when juvenile-court records are used as the measure of delinquency, 16 per cent of the non-college-prep students were delinquent dur-

TABLE 20. DIFFERENCE BETWEEN TRACKS IN DELINQUENCY RATE, %

	Total Delinquency Rate			
	Non-delinquent	*Delinquent*	*Total*	*N*
College-prep	94	6	100	(752)
Non-college-prep	84	16	100	(405)

	Delinquency Rate by Date of First Court Entry				
	Nondelinq.	*Delinq. before and during High School*	*Became Delinq. during High School*	*Total*	*N*
College-prep	94	1	5	100	(752)
Non-college-prep	84	5	11	100	(405)

ing high school, compared with less than half as high a percentage (6 per cent) of the college-prep students. This association held for boys and girls alike (see Table X in the Appendix). This finding may be the result of greater delinquency proneness in the first place among students who entered the non-college-prep track. However, when the analysis is limited to those students who did not have a court record before high school, the difference still remained, as shown in the lower portion of Table 20. More than twice as high a percentage of non-college-prep students became officially delinquent for the first time during high school. Simultaneous controls for father's occupation, IQ, and previous achievement did not eliminate this difference either, though they reduced it somewhat, as shown in Table 21. In Table 22, we see that track position related more strongly to delin-

TABLE 21. DIFFERENCE BETWEEN TRACKS IN DELINQUENCY RATE, STANDARDIZED FOR FATHER'S OCCUPATION, IQ, AND PREVIOUS ACHIEVEMENT, %*

	Nondelinquent	*Delinquent*	*Total*	*N*
College-prep	94	5	100	(708)
Non-college-prep	86	12	100	(354)

*This table and Table 22 include both those who were delinquent prior to high school and those who became delinquent during high school. The table is derived from Table IX in the Appendix.

TABLE 22. WEIGHTED MEAN DIFFERENCE IN DELINQUENCY RATE BY TRACK, PREVIOUS ACHIEVEMENT, IQ, AND FATHER'S OCCUPATION, %*

	Mean Difference
Track	8
Previous achievement	6
IQ	4
Father's occupation	3

*This table is derived from Table IX in the Appendix.

quency than did either father's occupation or IQ, two variables thought to be especially important as determinants of delinquency.

Delinquency may be largely a rebellion against the school and its standards (Cohen, 1955). At the least, being outside the mainstream of success and involvement in school may leave many students more open and susceptible to deviant influences. Our findings suggest that a key factor in rebellion and "drift" into delinquency which may be more important than working-class background is having a non-college-prep status in the school's track system, with the low achievement and marginal status that accompany that position.

This conclusion is consistent with the findings on the effect of streaming in a modern English secondary school:

> There is a real sense in which the school can be regarded as a generating factor of delinquency. Although the aims and efforts of the teachers are directed towards deleting such tendencies, the organization of the school and its influence on subcultural development unintentionally foster delinquent values .... For low stream boys ..., school simultaneously exposes them to these values and deprives them of status in these terms. It is at this point they may begin to reject the values because they cannot succeed in them. More than this, the school provides a mechanism through the streaming system whereby their failure is effected and institutionalized, and also provides a situation in which they can congregate together in low streams (Hargreaves, 1967, p. 173. New York: Humanities Press, Inc.).

SUMMARY

In the two Midwestern schools studied, non-college-prep students experienced lower academic achievement, greater decline and less improvement in achievement, less participation in extracurricular activities, greater misconduct in school, a greater tendency to drop out, and greater delinquency. It has been suggested that these differences were partly *caused* by factors associated with the student's position in the track system. Students from blue-collar and black families were disproportionately assigned to the non-college-prep track and were, therefore, more often subjected to the negative influences and relative disadvantages associated with that track.

We can only speculate about the generalizability of these findings to other schools. However, there is little reason to regard the two schools studied as especially unusual in relation to other schools in similar communities. Despite differences in the size and composition of the two student bodies, the findings were virtually identical and were consistent with the speculations, criticisms, and observations of many other writers.

To the extent the findings are valid and general, they lend support for the argument that, through tracking, the schools are partly causing many of the very problems they are trying to solve and are posing an important barrier to equal educational opportunity to lower-income and black students. The notion that schools foster low achievement, noncommitment and noninvolvement, dropping out, misconduct, and delinquency is foreign and repulsive to many teachers, administrators, and parents. Yet the evidence is consistent with Kai Erickson's observation that "deviant activities often seem to derive support from the very agencies designed to suppress them" (1964, p. 15).

CHAPTER 4

Interpretation of the Findings

Preceding chapters have described the track system as an organizational component of public high schools in the United States, and have presented the rationale on which the system is based. Then two schools which were studied were discussed, and the findings of the study were presented as a basis for determining whether or not the track system produces the beneficial effects it is assumed by many schoolmen to produce, or the negative consequences that its critics argue it produces. Since non-college-prep students experienced lower academic achievement, greater decline and less improvement in achievement, less participation in extracurricular activities, greater misconduct in school, a greater tendency to drop out before graduation, and greater delinquency than did college-prep students, it can be surmised that the track system may not produce the beneficial effects its rationale would lead one to expect and, further, that it produces several unintended negative consequences.

How can these findings be explained? What processes operated within the schools studied which were not taken into account in the rationale for tracking? Why did fewer non-college-prep students experience high academic achievement, academic improvement, and participation in extracurricular activities, while fewer college-prep students were involved in misconduct in school, dropped out, or became delinquent? While the data available for this study cannot provide definite answers, they do—in combination with findings from other studies, together with general behavioral-science theory—provide the basis for several plausible explanations. Since any observed social phenomenon is the result of the combined effect of several processes and since the findings in this study involve a variety of phenomena—academic achievement and improvement, extracurricular participation, dropping out, misconduct, delinquency, it might be argued that several processes, in combination, must have mediated between track position and the outcomes observed. In all probability, these processes included the self-fulfilling prophecy, track-related subcultures, the labeling process, different future payoffs, as well as differences in the quality of instruction and the development of personal commitment.

THE POSSIBILITY OF NO EFFECT

Although these processes probably operated in combination to bring about the variations in social and educational outcomes revealed by the study, it is also possible that the track-related differences were the product, not of track position at all, but of other selection factors or of extraneous influences. While there clearly is a *correlation* between track position and these outcomes, there might not be a *causal linkage* from the former to the latter. Rather, other factors which could not be measured or which were measured incompletely might be the real causes. Let us examine this interpretation more closely, since it has obvious plausibility.

What might some of these other factors be? One set of such influences can be grouped under the label "selection factors." It is entirely possible that students assigned to the college-prep track were brighter by nature, more skilled academically, and better motivated toward school and college when they entered high school. As noted in the previous chapter, such differences at the onset might result from influences associated with genetic inheritance, personality, the family, the peer group, or a host of other pre-high-school factors. That college-prep and non-college-prep students differed in achievement and conduct might then simply confirm the informed judgments of teachers and counselors who made the initial track-assignment decisions.

The selection interpretation could well be valid, at least in part. Even though the study sought to take it into account by statistically controlling for father's occupation, measured intelligence, and previous achievement, there is no question but that other selection differences by track position still remained. For instance, it is very likely that college-prep students in the upper range for father's occupation, IQ, and previous achievement to some degree still exceeded non-college-prep students within those same categories. Moreover, these three control variables clearly did not completely equate college-prep and non-college-prep students on prior differences having an effect on the outcomes measured. To be sure, the control for GPA from the last semester of junior high school must have captured many of these differences, but certainly not all of them.

Another alternative interpretation is that, even if students on the different tracks were in fact statistically equated on relevant factors at the point of entry, there were still extraneous, confounding, or outside influences operating simultaneously with track position that produced the results observed. For instance, it is possible that non-college-prep students were so distracted by cars, drugs, or the opposite sex that their grades, attitudes, involvement, and behavior suffered. This argument also is plausible although, as we shall see, many of these "extraneous" factors (such as peer influence) may not have been extraneous at all, but themselves partly caused by the track system.

The question is not whether selection or extraneous factors contributed to the reported outcomes; it is almost certain that they did. The real questions are: How much difference did track position make? And why?

It is entirely understandable that teachers who seek to do a good job within the track system regard underachievement, negative attitudes, and misconduct as the result of factors inherent in the pupils or their families rather than in the school. Such an interpretation easily follows from the individualistic, rather than systemic, world view which affects socialization in Western, capitalistic, Protestant countries.

In fact, this interpretation was prevalent in the two schools studied:

> Three-fifths or more of the teachers in the schools studied [three others were included besides Industrial City and Academic Heights] reported that the single most important source of difficulty for most or all malperformers was their lack of motivation and interest in school. Motivation was thought to be an attribute that the pupil brought to school, and few teachers indicated an awareness of ways in which educational practices in school contribute to it (Sarri and Vinter, 1969, p. 111).

Another study found that the home was most often blamed (Hargreaves, 1967). While the investigation found home-related differences (for example, the higher the stream, the higher the parents' occupational aspirations for the son and the more severe their attitudes toward low academic achievement), it concluded that the family-background interpretation by itself was oversimplified:

> It was common practice for the teachers to shed the blame for many difficulties which might be caused or reinforced by the school itself on to the home environment. Yet the belief that children are "difficult" in school *because* they come from "difficult" homes is a convenient oversimplification. At Lumley, the misbehavior of low stream boys was often "explained" by the teachers in terms of a popular psychology or sociology. A teacher once re-

marked to me, "Well, what can you expect? That lad's got no father"—but he failed to appreciate that the most hardworking member of the "intellectual" B clique in 4A was also fatherless (Hargreaves, 1967, p. 183. New York: Humanities Press, Inc.).

Thus, while selection and extraneous factors might partly account for the differences in educational outcomes reported in the previous chapter, and while all possible factors may not have been taken into account, there remains a strong likelihood that these outcomes were largely caused by factors associated with track position itself. The following sections will discuss the mediating processes found in previous studies and suggested by general social-science theory which, in combination, provide an explanation for the findings of this study.

THE SELF-FULFILLING PROPHECY

It is likely that non-college-prep students were low in motivation, commitment to school, grades, involvement, conformity, and attendance partly *because* teachers, counselors, and others expected them to be that way. In short, these students were probably ensnared in a negative self-fulfilling prophecy.

The idea of the self-fulfilling prophecy is very old. It is rooted in the assumption that an individual's conception of himself, his abilities, his identity, his sense of worth, and his behavior is partly determined by how other people define him.[1] If, for example, his parents believe a child to be a dullard, he not only will come to see himself as dull but in fact will probably become so, because of how he is treated, addressed, and expected to behave.

There is growing evidence that the self-fulfilling prophecy operates in the school as well as elsewhere. Convincing evidence that teachers get what they expect—that students become what they are expected to become—may be found in a study by Rosenthal and Jacobson (1968). Here the influence was positive. In late spring, all of the children in an elementary school who would be returning in the fall were given a test allegedly designed to identify "intellectual spurting potential" among about 20 per cent of the students. The experimenters were the only ones who knew that the test was simply a standardized test of intelligence. The following fall, 20 per cent of the children in each classroom were randomly assigned to the experimental group of "spurters." While their teachers were told to expect rapid intellectual

[1]For a review of the history of the idea as it pertains to the classroom, see Rosenthal and Jacobson (1968).

gains during the ensuing months, the teachers were told nothing about the control group. The only "experimental input," in other words, was the list of names of the children in the experimental group. As predicted, the experimental group showed significantly greater gains in IQ and grades after one semester, one year, and two years than did the control group. Further, they were rated by the teachers as being significantly more curious, interesting, happy, and more likely to succeed in the future. While the younger children changed the most during the first year, the changes persisted into the second year to a greater extent for older children. Equally significant was the fact that ratings were most negative for control-group children on the low track who were not expected to gain but did so.

Although the investigators had no way of determining the precise psychological and interpersonal processes mediating between teacher expectations and student performance, they suggested that subtle, unintended, and unrecognized differences in communication accounted for the effect. Despite certain limitations in the study (such as the unaccountably low pretest IQ scores and the fact that teachers soon forgot who the experimental children were), it has provided strong evidence that the self-fulfilling prophecy operates between teachers and students. The findings of this study lend credence to the position expressed by many critics and investigators during the past decade that low teacher expectations partly account for the low level of performance by disadvantaged students. The HARYOU report, for example, states:

> On the evidence available to date, it must be concluded the major reason why an increasing number of central Harlem pupils fall behind in their grade level is that substandard performance is expected of them (*Youth in the Ghetto*, 1964, p. 237).

Similarly, another observer has remarked:

> Not infrequently teachers, counsellors, principals assigned to the depressed area schools have been people without any real concern for these children and with the common stereotype of them as children of low ability. As a result of this low estimate of potential, the self-fulfilling prophecy went into effect. The children were not encouraged to learn very much; the teacher expended little energy on anything but maintaining order and bemoaning her lot; as a consequence, the children fulfilled the lowest expectations, which in turn enforced the original assumption to prove that the teacher was right (Ravitz, 1963, p. 19).

The findings by Rosenthal and Jacobson add plausibility to the assertion that the self-fulfilling prophecy contributed to the outcomes revealed in the findings of the present study. Unfortunately, there are no systematic measures of teacher expectations for this study. However, the evidence from another study strongly suggests that teachers of non-college-prep students probably harbor lower expectations:

In a streamed school the teacher categorizes the pupils not only in terms of the inferences he makes from the child's classroom behavior but also from the child's stream level. It is for this reason that the teacher can rebuke an A stream boy for behaving like a D stream boy. The teacher has learned to *expect* certain kinds of behavior from members of different streams.

Perhaps the most important and only partially recognized effect of categorization is the way in which this process sets up counterexpectations in the pupil. Because a teacher has categorized a pupil, however provisionally, he may in his own behavior toward the pupil emit expectations to which the relatively immature pupil will conform. This by-product of categorization will be most marked at the extremes, that is, with the "good" and "bad" pupils. It would hardly be surprising if "good" pupils thus become "better" and the "bad" pupils become "worse." It is, in short, an example of a self-fulfilling prophecy. The negative expectations of the teacher reinforce the negative behavioural tendencies.

It is important to stress that if this effect of categorization is real, it is entirely unintended by the teachers. They do not wish to make low streams more difficult than they are! (Hargreaves, 1967, pp. 105–106. New York: Humanities Press, Inc.)

Tracking, like streaming, may well generate self-fulfilling differences in teacher expectations by the very nature of the categories and labels employed, despite the best intentions of individual teachers. Another writer argues that tracking has damaging effects on teachers as well as on pupils:

Tracking, or homogeneous grouping by ability, is bad not only because of its effects upon students; it also has an insidious and destructive effect upon teachers. Where children are grouped by ability, teachers often do not appreciate and may even resent the effort of a low-track student who tries to improve. From the teacher's standpoint, it is almost as if a low-track, supposedly unmotivated student has no business changing (Glasser, 1969, p. 82).

This view is consistent with the labeling theory of deviant behavior (Schafer, 1967).

One way the self-fulfilling prophecy, beginning with teacher expectations, has its effects is through its influence on the student's self-esteem. A substantial literature has developed in recent years showing that high academic performance is associated with high esteem (Brookover and Gottlieb, 1964) and that individuals develop loyalty and commitment to a group or organization to the extent that the group generates in the person positive feelings about himself (Katz and Kahn, 1966). A number of writers have contended that the low expectations by teachers of students in the low-ability group or non-college-prep track probably have a dampening effect on self-esteem. One of them has made the following observations about the connections between grouping, self-esteem, and intellectual growth.

The teacher learns that [the student] has a low IQ rating and puts him into a slow-moving group where he is not expected to do much or be given much attention. He is bright enough, however, to catch on very quickly to the fact that he is not considered very bright. He comes to accept this very unflattering appraisal because, after all, the school should know. He is in his pigeon hole. He can't get out, and what is more, he doesn't try; he accepts his fate. His parents accept it, since, after all, the schools should know. Intellectually, he is lost. He has accepted this low appraisal of himself; and both he and society must suffer the consequences (Sexton, 1961, p. 52).

Another observer describes this process in different terms:

The general course (meaning the dead end) and the vocational track are composed of the sons and daughters of blue-collar workers. The more "opportunity," the more justified the destiny of those who are tagged for failure. The world accepts the legitimacy of their position. And so do they. Their tragedy and the accompanying threat lie precisely in their acceptance of the low esteem in which school, society, and often their parents regard them, and in their inability to learn a language to express what they feel but dare not trust (Schrag, 1970, p. 60).

Several studies provide systematic evidence in support of this description (Frease, 1969; Kelly, 1970).

Still another writer has pointed out that the self-fulfilling prophecy associated with tracking or streaming is similar in its effects to that associated with categorization by IQ (Elder, 1965). Illustrative is the following anecdote by Dr. Samuel Shepard, director of the Banneker project in St. Louis:

. . . here was a teacher who had copied the IQ numbers down the line from a list in the principal's office. . . . throughout the semester if the teacher called on Mary, let us say with an IQ of 119, she followed somewhat this pattern: if Mary didn't respond quickly, "Well, now, come on, Mary. You know you can do this. You know how we did this yesterday"; or bring up an analogous situation. She encouraged, she stimulated, until Mary came up with the proper answer, or what the teacher at least considered an adequate one. However, when she called on poor John with his 74 IQ, if he mumbled something fairly audible, why this was wonderful; pat him on the back and "Be sure and be here tomorrow. You can work the windows and help move the piano and water the flowers, and the erasers must be washed," and so forth. This is teaching by IQ. She was a little horrified at the end of the semester when she turned in her grades. She looked under the glass and saw that the columns she had copied for IQ's were locker numbers. (Wallace Mendelson,

Discrimination. Based on the Report of the United States Commission on Civil Rights, © 1962, Prentice-Hall, Inc. P. 54.)

Interviews in the two schools of the present study suggested that the self-fulfilling prophecy was formalized or institutionalized by the operation of grade ceilings for non-college-prep students and grade floors for college-bound students. By virtue of being located in a college-prep section or course, a student could seldom earn any grade lower than B or C, while a student in a non-college-prep section or course found it difficult to gain any grade higher than C, even though his objective performance may have been equivalent to a college-prep B. Several teachers explicitly called our attention to this practice, the rationale being that non-college-prep students do not "deserve" the same objective grade rewards as do college-prep students, since they "clearly" are less bright and perform less well. To the extent that grade ceilings did operate for non-college-bound students, lower grades were simply further assured by the absence of available potential rewards for achievement, with resulting deterioration of motivation and commitment.

In short, then, track position may have affected academic achievement, involvement, conformity, and persistence in school, as well as delinquency, partly because the negative expectations by teachers of non-college-prep students in turn led to a deterioration of commitment, motivation, self-esteem, performance, and conduct. While further evidence is needed, the literature and arguments just cited support the validity of the argument that the self-fulfilling process was an important part of the over-all social and educational dynamic in the schools studied.

TRACK-RELATED SUBCULTURES

In the previous section, it was suggested that the track system affected students partly through its influence on the expectations and behavior of teachers. Another, complementary process relates to the mediating influence of peers. It is contended that the track system itself helps generate track-linked student subcultures which tend either to support or to oppose the official culture of the school (for example, that students should work for good grades and should obey school rules) and that these subcultures in turn affect the educational outcomes of particular students.

Considerable effort has been invested in studying the nature and sources of youth subculture in the schools of the United States. An important contribution of one of the most significant of those studies was to develop the argument that the structure of the school itself helps determine the types of values, norms, and attitudes developed and shared by students (Coleman, 1961). Specifically, the study contended that the individualistic, competitive structure of academics helps generate norms against high academic achievement, since one man's gain is another's loss when a limited supply of high grades is available. While the study also found differences in the nature of peer subcultures (for example, emphasis on going to college), it did not develop the idea that a single school structure might generate different student subcultures within the same school. It is the contention here that the formal track system gives rise both to educationally supportive subcultures (in the case of college-prep students) and to educationally antagonistic subcultures (in the case of non-college-prep students). Moreover, the initiation of students into these subcultures helps account for the track-related differences in educational outcomes shown in the previous chapter.

The best evidence for this claim again comes from the study of Lumley School in England (Hargreaves, 1967). Assignment to a lower stream at Lumley meant that a boy was immediately immersed in a student subculture which stressed and rewarded antagonistic attitudes and behavior toward teachers and all they stood for. If a boy was assigned to the "A" stream, he was drawn toward the values of teachers, not only by the higher expectations and more positive rewards from teachers themselves, but by other students as well. The converse was true of lower-stream boys, who accorded one another high status for doing the *opposite* of what teachers wanted. Because of class scheduling, little opportunity developed for interaction and friendship across streams, with negative stereotyping developing instead. The results were a progressive polarization and hardening of the high- and low-stream subcultures between the first and fourth years and a progressively greater negative attitude between streams, with quite predictable consequences:

> The informal pressures within the low streams tend to work directly against the assumption of the teachers that boys will regard promotion into a higher stream as a desirable goal. The boys from the low streams were very reluctant to ascend to higher streams because their stereotypes of "A" and "B" stream boys were defined in terms of values alien to their own and because promotion would involve rejection by their low stream friends. The teachers were not fully aware that this unwillingness to be promoted to a higher stream led high informal status boys to depress their performance in

examinations. This fear of promotion adds to our list of factors leading to the formation of anti-academic attitudes among low stream boys (Hargreaves, 1967, p. 77. New York: Humanities Press, Inc.).

Hargreaves pointed out that the stream-related peer-group norms had an independent influence on delinquency outside the school as well as on within-school performance and behavior. The following discussion highlights not only this fact, but also the intricate interconnections between influences from home and the streaming system of the school:

> Although part of the explanation for the lack of delinquency in the A stream derives from the home background, this is not in itself a sufficient explanation. . . . The factor we wish to stress here is the pressure in the peer group. The norms in 4A would *necessarily* have to proscribe delinquent behavior, since this would be inconsistent with the other predominating norms, which advocated behaviour in conformity with the teachers' expectations. To accept and internalize the teachers' values is to reject delinquent behavior. "Good lads do not steal." Such support for these values as comes from the home will act in two ways. It will *predispose* boys to accepting the teachers' role expectations and to being integrated into the A stream, and it will *reinforce* the group's own norms. Likewise, where neither the group nor the home prohibit delinquent behavior, the focus will draw the boys toward delinquency. In those cases where the home influence is not sharply defined in this respect, the peer group norms will become increasingly powerful in determining the attitude and values and behaviour of the boy (Hargreaves, 1967, p. 111. New York: Humanities Press, Inc.).

A study of adolescents in the state of Oregon suggests that similar processes occur in United States schools as well (Frease, 1969). Not only were the levels of self-esteem, attitudes toward school, and academic achievement lower among non-college-bound students but also rates of delinquency and friendship with delinquent individuals were higher. The study drew on both delinquency theory and more general social-psychological theory to suggest the development out of the formal track system of track-related antagonistic or supportive peer subcultures. The findings are consistent with those of numerous other studies cited earlier on the effect of peers on educational and occupational aspirations and expectations.

Observations and unstructured interviews in the schools studied for this volume confirmed a polarization similar to that at Lumley and a comparable reluctance by non-college-prep students to pursue seriously the academic goals rewarded by teachers and college-prep students. Closer examination probably also would have shown similar differences in pressures toward or away from participation in extracurricular activities, conformity to school rules, and persistence in school through graduation.

THE LABELING SYNDROME

Another reason for the negative educational outcomes of non-college-prep students may well be that assignment to this track confers on students a stigmatizing label which in turn erodes self-esteem and commitment to the goals and norms of the school. Organizations in the business of trying to change people frequently label and stigmatize certain types of individuals whom they "process." There is also evidence that externally imposed labels or stigmas often are either internalized or rebelled against. On the one hand, the ex-convict comes to see himself as just that—with no hope that reform will dispel the label; his sense of identity is shaped by that label alone. The same is true of the alcoholic or the drug addict. Predictably, such a person tends to take on the role, behavior, and public image which fit the conception he and others have of himself. He is also increasingly likely to regard himself with less and less esteem and worth. On the other hand, in time, the person so labeled grows to resent the label and to strike back at those who have labeled and otherwise wronged him. His resentment may generalize to the whole system they represent and of which they are a part.

These subtle but real processes involve not only the individual who has been stigmatized or labeled, but also his interactions with his social environment (Becker, 1963, 1964). He enters a social category, perhaps not of his own volition. The label attached to that category attaches to him as a person. If the label carries with it a negative stigma, he becomes a stigmatized human being. Others come to view him not so much as John Jones, a unique person, but as an occupant of that category, a type of person. They treat him accordingly, perhaps unintentionally. He in turn finds himself coming to believe the label, accepting the stigma, viewing himself as a lesser person. His level and quality of behavior or performance may decline along the way as his expectations of himself gradually deteriorate. He is likely to turn toward other, less humiliating activities and situations, frequently seeking and finding others with a similar plight. Together they reinforce each other in their antagonism toward the system that stigmatized them, and together they pursue other, more attainable and satisfying goals.

Recently, this interactional or labeling perspective has been applied to analysis of the school as well, with the result that attention is directed not only at failures, alienated youth, and troublemakers but also at the interactions, or processes, which occur between them and others in the system. One such analysis has provided an incisive and penetrating description of the stigmatizing process among gang members in an urban school (Werthman, 1967). Similarly, another study has pointed out some of the negative effects of the stigma attached to failure and deviant behavior, with the consequences for the self-esteem, commitment, and later behavior of high-school youth (Schafer and Polk, 1967).

Thus, labeling may be considered an important process in producing the negative personal, educational, and behavioral effects of assignment to the non-college-prep track. Numerous writers have noted the negative evaluation attached to the non-college-prep track (B. Clark, 1962; Stinchcombe, 1964; Thomas and Thomas, 1965; Tanner, 1965; Sexton, 1961; Venn, 1964). Many have remarked on the corroding effects of this stigma on self-esteem. As one high-school boy bemoaned, "around here you are *nothing* if you're not college prep" (Mallery, 1962).

Unstructured interviews in the two schools studied clearly suggested that stigma indeed went along with the non-college-prep track. A non-college-prep girl told one of the authors that she always carried her general-track books upside-down to make them less identifiable, because of the humiliation she felt when other students saw them as she walked through the halls. Unfortunately, status differences, or undesired labels, cannot be so easily hidden or stigma so readily wished away. A former delinquent interviewed by one of the authors in Washington, D.C., put it well:

It really don't have to be the tests, but after the tests, there shouldn't be no separation in the classes. Because, as I say again, I felt good when I was with my class, but when they went and separated us—that changed us. That changed our ideas, our thinking, the way we thought about each other and turned us to enemies toward each other—because they said I was dumb and they were smart (Schafer and Polk, 1967, p. 241).

The damaging effects on this boy's sense of worth and potential were clear:

When you first go to junior high school you do feel something inside—it's like a ego. You have been from elementary to junior high, you feel great inside. You say, well daggone, I'm going to deal with the *people* here now, I am in junior high school. You get this shirt that says Brown Junior High or whatever the name is and you are proud of that shirt. But then you go up there and the teacher say—"well, so and so, you're in the basic section, you can't go with the other kids." The devil with the whole thing—you lose—something in you—like it just goes out of you.

(Did you think the other guys were smarter than you?) Not at first—I used to think I was just as smart as anybody in the school—I felt it inside of me. When the first year into junior high school—I knew I was smart. I knew some people were smarter, but I knew I could be just as good as they were—and I wanted to go to school, I wanted to get a diploma and go to college and help people and everything. I stepped into there in junior high—I felt like a fool going to school—I really felt like a fool. (Why?) Because I felt like I wasn't a part of the school. I couldn't get on special patrols, because I wasn't qualified.

(What happened between the seventh and ninth grades?) I started losing faith in myself—after the teachers kept downing me, you know. You hear "a guy's in basic section, he's dumb" and all this. Each year—"you're ignorant—you're stupid" (Schafer and Polk, 1967, pp. 241–242).

Non-college-prep students are denied not only status but also opportunities to become engaged in prestigious and rewarding activities:

(What happened after you were separated? You said you didn't have any opportunities any more. What kind?) I mean—they'd get special things. When you're ready to graduate from junior high, you get to take pictures and go on picnics and stuff. Basic classes don't do this. You don't get to take any pictures in basic classes. You don't get a chance to be in the recital, you don't get the chance to do certain things. You know, 9–7, 9–8, and 9–9, they gave a big play. But none of the basic section was included, although we was classified as the ninth grade (Schafer and Polk, 1967, p. 242).

The direct connection between track position and delinquency can hardly be better illustrated than in this excerpt:

You can't get on this, you can't get on that and the girls that were in my class back in the sixth grade—they look at you—"you're in the basic section aren't you." You know, all of a sudden the guys you used to hang out with won't hang out with you no more. They hang out with a new class of people. Like they're classifying themselves as middle class and you're low brow and, you know, you start feeling bad and I said I can prove that I'm middle class and I don't have to go to school to prove it. And so I did. I got out of school. All those kids' mothers buying them nice things in ninth and tenth grades. I said, baby, you ain't talking about nothing—and what your mother has to buy you I can get everyday. I used to sport around. Yeah—I used to show them $125—*every* day. I used to say—you have to go on to school for 12 years and I only went for 9. (How did you get this money?) I'd take it. (How did you take it?) I broke into things. I used to have a little racket set up. I used to have a protection fee—anybody who wants to cross the street, anybody who wants to come into my territory, they has to pay me 25 cents. I gave boys certain areas where they couldn't cross. A cat used to live up there. I say, "okay that's your deadline right there. If you want to go through this way, you give me 25 cents. If I ever catch you coming down through this way, you got a fight on your hands." And they gave me 25 cents (Schafer and Polk, 1967, p. 242).

In summary, then, non-college-prep students in this study of two high schools had lower academic achievement, declining grades, less participation in extracurricular activities, greater misconduct in school, greater delinquency, and a higher dropout rate partly because the stigma attached to them as occupants of an "inferior" social category generated low self-esteem, declining commitment to school, and progressively greater withdrawal, rebellion, and turning away. While the data preclude a systematic evaluation of whether or not this process was a fundamental influence in the schools studied, stigmatization is likely to have complemented and become intertwined with the other mediating processes described in this chapter.

DIFFERENT FUTURE PAYOFFS

The non-college-prep students in this study were likely to have developed progressively more negative attitudes and behavior toward school partly because they saw grades, conformity, involvement, and indeed staying in school until graduation as having little payoff in the future. For the college-prep student, good grades, staying out of trouble, and accumulating a good record did seem important for the future. For them, these are means toward the identifiable and meaningful end of qualifying for college, although increasing numbers of middle-class college-bound students are now questioning whether they really want to play that game after all. But for the non-college-bound student, far less future payoff could be expected from good grades and a good record since they will have little to do with getting a blue-collar job or attending a vocational school.

This difference in the instrumental importance of conformity, involvement, and achievement is magnified by the perception on the part of the non-college-bound student that schoolwork is unrelated in terms of content or skills to what he will be doing on the job. A study of high-school rebelliousness came to a similar conclusion about the alienating effects of the ineffective articulation of the connection between the high-school career and the later occupational career among non-college-bound students:

> . . . rebellion . . . occurs when future status is not closely related to present performance. When a student realizes that he has not achieved status increment from improved current performance, current performance loses meaning. The student becomes hedonistic because he does not visualize achievement of long run goals through current self-constraint. He reacts negatively to a conformity that offers nothing concrete. He claims autonomy from adults because their authority does not promise a satisfactory future (Stinchcombe, 1964, p. 5).

> The major practical conclusion of the analysis above is that rebellious behavior is largely a reaction to the school itself and to its promises, not a failure of the family or community. High school students can be motivated to conform by paying them in the realistic coin of future advantage. Except perhaps for pathological cases, any student can be motivated to conform if the school can realistically promise something valuable to him as a reward for working hard. But for a large part of the population, especially the adolescent who will enter the male working class or the female candidates for early marriage, the school has nothing to offer. . . . In order to secure conformity from students, the high school must articulate academic work with careers of students (Stinchcombe, 1964, p. 179).

Another former delinquent in Washington, D.C., told one of the authors how the perceived lack of future payoff affected him personally:

> (What kind of school program were you doing? Vocational education?) Yeah, vocational training. (Did that prepare you for a job?) It was supposed to prepare me for a job but it didn't. (Did you try to get a job?) Yeah, I tried to get a job. The men said I wasn't qualified. (Did you think while you were in school that you would get a job?) That's right—that's why I stayed in school so I could get a job upon completion of high school because they put so much emphasis on getting a high school diploma. "If you get a high school diploma, you can do this and you can do this, without it you can't do this." And I got one and I still can't do nothing. I can't get a job or nothing, after I got one (Schafer and Polk, 1967, p. 246).

The deep disillusionment felt by such youth produces not only shattered hopes, but also a damaged sense of self-worth, a declining interest in school, and the attraction to other activities, some of which may run counter to school authorities or the law. As to the dropout problem, "Why bother to stay in school when graduation for half of the boys opens onto a dead-end street?" (Conant, 1961, p. 33.) Further, experiences and attitudes like those of this youth are communicated to younger brothers and sisters, to neighbors and friends, sometimes inducing a negative stance before they even enter high school. Lack of future payoff may help explain not only the findings of the sample studied, but also similar patterns for later generations of students.

DIFFERENT QUALITY OF INSTRUCTION

Still another interpretation of the findings is that teachers of non-college-prep students did a less effective and stimulating job than they did with college-prep students. It is no secret that most teachers look with disdain on teaching low-ability groups or non-college-prep students. There is evidence that teachers in a variety of geographical and community settings shared the strong preference not to teach lower-track students ("Teacher Opinion Poll," 1968). Interestingly enough, there is also some evidence, at least in English schools, that less–qualified, less–experienced, and less–effective teachers are more often assigned to low-ability or non-college-prep classes. Some of the subtle effects at Lumley were described as follows:

Since all teachers are 'tested out' by pupils to see 'how far they can go', pupils with less strict teachers will build up different concepts of acceptable behaviour to boys with more strict teachers. The policy of placing lower streams under the supervision of less competent and less strict teachers has the effect of giving these pupils extended expectations about the kind of behaviour which will be tolerated from them, and thus of granting the high status pupils even greater control over the deviant behaviour which in any case becomes normative in lower streams by the fourth year. The school's method of allocating teachers may thus reinforce those processes by which lower stream pupils deviate increasingly from the school's expectations as they progress through their four years at Lumley (Hargreaves, 1967, p. 98. New York: Humanities Press, Inc.).

The less competent teachers who tend to be assigned to low streams are faced with much more difficult problems than their colleagues with high streams. At Lumley, low stream teachers adapt to their situation in two basic ways. The first mode of adaptation is that of *withdrawal*. Because this type of teacher is less competent in matters of discipline yet is assigned to forms with the greatest discipline problems, he avoids the problem by ignoring its existence. He does this by sitting in his desk at the front, marking boys' work or some similar activity, whilst the rest of the class continue to enjoy the relative chaos which reigns. The class members are frequently at different stages in each subject so that no check can be made on individual or group progress. Alternatively, withdrawal can take the form of lecturing to the class in a voice sufficiently loud to drown the voices of misbehaving pupils. In this way the teacher appears to be teaching, even though the pupils complete little work. The second mode of adaptation for the less competent teachers with low streams is that of *domination*. This type of teacher imposes a completely rigid discipline, infringements of which incur severe penalties. Because silence reigns in the form, the children appear to be working hard. In reality, they make little effort; they become increasingly bored by the lesson, their interest in the subject declines, and they seek to undermine the authority of the teacher by disturbing the lesson without being apprehended (Hargreaves, 1967, pp. 103–104. New York: Humanities Press, Inc.).

From what is known about the reciprocal interaction between teacher and class, low teacher effectiveness in non-college-prep tracks may result from the attitudes and collective stance of low-track students as much as from initial low levels of competence or enthusiasm by the teacher. Even when the same individual teaches classes on both tracks during a day or week (as was true for most teachers in the two schools studied), he is likely to be "up" for college-prep classes and "down" for non-college-prep classes, partly as a predictable reaction to the dominant positive or negative climate among the students. The teacher's mood, enthusiasm, and effectiveness in turn are likely to reverberate on the students.

The Development of Personal Commitment

Finally, it is possible that the outcomes resulted from an entirely intrapersonal process: once an individual made a decision at the beginning of high school to go to college, his commitment to the official norms of the school and to the standards and expectations of teachers increased or crystallized. Not only do subsequent grades become instrumental, but also a "good record" in terms of conduct and participation becomes important for the college-bound youth. Moreover, a greater identification with teachers and the educational process generally is likely to follow. On the other hand, non-college-prep students have less to gain and less reason to develop a strong identification with the school or the teachers. This interpretation is consistent with dissonance theory: once a personal decision is made, future attitudes and behavior will be congruent with it, especially when the initial decision involves a public behavioral commitment, such as occupancy of a social position like college-prep or non-college-prep track.[2]

Summary

This chapter has been addressed to the question: *Why* do non-college-prep students experience lower academic achievement,

[2]See, for example, Festinger (1957, 1964), Abelson *et al.* (1968).

greater decline and less improvement in achievement, less participation in extracurricular activities, greater misconduct in school, a greater tendency to drop out before graduation, and greater delinquency? While the data do not permit a direct empirical answer, earlier research and theory in the behavioral sciences and in education indicate several explanatory processes which, in combination, might account for the findings.

It is entirely possible that the relationships between track position and educational outcomes, described in the preceding chapter, were correlational but not causal and that part or all of the outcomes were simply the result of selection or extraneous influences rather than track position. However, the question is not whether selection or simultaneous confounding factors contributed to the reported outcomes; almost certainly, they did. The real questions are: How much difference did track position make? And why? The lack of complete control over all other possible influences made it impossible to assess fully the relative impact of track position, but it is contended that the data strongly suggest some, and perhaps even considerable, effect on educational outcomes.

A further contention is that this independent effect occurs through the operation of several mediating processes. Among them is the self-fulfilling prophecy, in which teachers of the non-college-prep track expect less and get less. This hypothesis is consistent with general knowledge of the interactional process as well as with studies of the effects of teacher expectation on pupil performance, attitudes, and behavior.

A second process which is consistent both with the understanding of peer influence in general and with research on streaming in English schools is that the college-prep track generates a generally proschool student subculture, while the non-college-prep track generates a negative, antischool subculture which is passed on from one generation of students to the next and exerts on students who enter it an independent influence away from official school goals and norms.

The labeling interpretation holds that the negative evaluations and low public esteem directed at non-college-prep students by other students and by teachers leads to a deterioration of self-esteem, aspirations, and educational commitment. In addition, research suggests that non-college-prep students fall behind, rebel, and turn away more often because they fail to see much prospect of future payoff for present conformity and achievement.

The findings probably resulted in part from differences between tracks in the level of interest, energy, and instructional quality by teachers. Even when teachers spend time in both types of classes, as was true at the two high schools studied, they are more likely to be "up" in college-prep classes and "down" in basic, vocational, or general classes or sections—bringing out the same response in their students. Finally, the degree of personal commitment of students to their schools was considered to have varied between college-prep and non-college-prep students. Once a student makes a decision to go to college, his subsequent attitudes, behavior, and performance are likely to be consistent and in accord with official school norms and with teacher expectations. On the other hand, students who do not commit themselves to the goal of college are less likely to consider conformity to school norms and teacher expectations very important.

All of these processes probably combined and interacted with one another to produce the results reported in the preceding chapter. The precise amount and form of influence of each set of factors can only be determined through multivariate research on the mediating processes at work.

CHAPTER 5

Implications: Beyond the Track System

In the two Midwestern high schools studied, non-college-prep students exhibited notably higher rates of academic failure, academic decline, noninvolvement in extracurricular activities, misbehavior, dropout, and delinquency, even after the effects of several influences other than track position were controlled. The claim is made that these associations are not just correlational but are causal. The previous chapter discussed several mediating processes that might explain these relationships.

That these findings can be generalized to other schools is a matter for speculation. However, there is little reason to believe that the two schools studied were unusual or unrepresentative of schools of similar size, composition, and community setting. Despite differences in size and social-class composition, the findings are virtually identical. Furthermore, they are consistent with the speculations, criticisms, and qualitative observations of numerous writers, as well as with the results of comparable observations in English schools. At the very least, these data suggest a need for further research, based on a larger sample and including a greater number of control and intervening variables. But to the extent that the findings are valid and general (despite the limitations stated in Chapter 2), they suggest that, through the track system, the schools are partly causing many of the very problems of student alienation, rebellion, and failure they are trying to solve. The schools themselves are posing a barrier to equal educational opportunity for lower-income and minority-group students, who are disproportionately assigned to the non-college-prep track.

THE THEORETICAL IMPLICATIONS

What are the theoretical implications to be derived from this study? The findings lend support to two important propositions at higher levels of abstraction. At the level of general organizational theory, the results provide further confirmation of the proposition, already supported by a growing body of literature, that the processes and programs created by people-changing organizations have a vital impact on their outcomes. At the level of the sociology of educational organizations, the findings offer further evidence that schools indeed affect student performance and behavior. While at first glance these propositions may appear trite or obvious, they have been the object of much debate, confusion, and research. As recently as 1966, the Coleman report concluded that school variables have little relative impact on educational outcomes (Coleman *et al.*, 1966).

The theoretical and practical import of these propositions is indeed great, for they direct the attention of both the researcher and the schoolman to influences within as well as outside the organization. While external factors affecting students, clients, inmates, or patients cannot be ignored in designing a theory or program, it is increasingly clear that influences internal to the organization's program and patterns of interaction must be taken into account. In the words of Fantini and Weinstein (1968), the focus becomes the organization's *process*, not the initial defects or liabilities in the eventual *product*. Later in this chapter it will be argued that in the case of the school the organization's *purpose* also needs to be questioned. The challenge confronting the organizational or educational theorist then becomes one of designing models and studies for systematically investigating the impact of other school-related factors as well.

THE EDUCATIONAL IMPLICATIONS

The implications of this study for educational policy and practice are considerably more complex. Some might argue that, despite the negative side effects which have been revealed, track systems are essential for effective teaching, especially for students with high ability or aspiration levels, as well as for adjusting students early in their careers to the status levels they will occupy in the adult occupational system. However reasonable this rationale may sound, the negative effects demonstrated offset and call into serious question any presumed gains from tracking.

Others might counter that the negative outcomes documented by this study can be eliminated by raising teacher expectations of non-college-prep students, making concerted efforts to reduce the stigma attached to non-college-prep classes, assigning good teachers to non-college-prep classes, rewarding teachers for doing an effective job of stimulating their students, and developing fair and equitable grading practices in both college-prep and non-college-prep classes.

Attractive as they may appear, efforts like these are apt to be fruitless so long as track systems—and indeed schools as they now exist—remain fundamentally unchanged. What is needed are wholly new, experimental environments of teaching-learning-living, even outside the schools if necessary. The schools of the future must address themselves to two major problems highlighted by the findings: (1) ensuring equality of opportunity for students now "locked out" by tracking, and (2) offering—to all students—a far more fulfilling and satisfying learning experience.

Equality of Opportunity

One approach to building greater equality of opportunity into existing or new secondary schools is the New Careers model (Pearl and Reissman, 1965). This model, which provides for fundamentally different linkages between educational and occupational careers, is based on the recognition that present options for entering the world of work are narrowly limited: the individual either acquires a high-school diploma and goes to work or he first goes to college and perhaps then to a graduate or professional school.

The New Careers model provides for new options. The youth who does not want to attend college, or who would not qualify according to usual criteria, is given the opportunity to attend high school part-time while working in a lower-level position in an expanded professional career hierarchy (including such new positions as teacher aide and teacher associate in education). Such a person would then have the options of moving up through progressively more demanding educational and work stages; and moving back and forth between the work place, the high school, and then the college. As ideally conceived, this model would allow able and aspiring persons ultimately to progress to the level of the fully certified teacher, nurse, librarian, social worker, or public administrator. While the New Careers model has been developed and tried primarily in the human-service sector of the economy, it is also applicable to the industrial and business sector as well (Schafer and Polk, 1967).

This alternative means of linking education with work has a number of advantages: students can try different occupations while still in school; students can earn while studying; they can spend more time outside the four walls of the school, learning what can best be learned in the work place; less stigma will accrue to those not immediately college-bound, since they too will have a future; studying and learning will be inherently more relevant because it will relate to a career in which they are actively involved; teachers of such students will be less likely to develop lower expectations because these youth too will have an unlimited, open-ended future; and antischool subcultures will be less likely to develop, since education will not be as negative, frustrating, or stigmatizing.

Enjoyment in Education

To ensure equality of opportunity is not enough. Merely to open the channels for lower-income youth to flow into educational careers that are now disappointing millions of middle-class college-bound youth is hardly a progressive step forward. Though not reflected in the data of this study, many middle-class students currently find school even less tolerable than do low-income youth. The empty grade-scrambling, teacher-pleasing, and stultifying passivity such youth must endure stand in greater and greater contrast to their home and other nonschool environments, which usually yield much greater excitement, challenge, and reward. More and more are dropping out psychologically, turning instead to drugs, apathy, or political activism, often of an unthinking and self-defeating kind.

What is needed, then, are entirely new and different models that will ensure equality of opportunity but also much more in the way of an enriching and rewarding process of growth. Educational environments of the future, incorporating the New Careers model as well as other new forms, must follow several simple principles.

First, successful new learning environments must be based on the recognition and nurturance of each individual's uniqueness. Each person must be allowed and stimulated to develop, learn, and grow as an individual, not as a standardized occupant of one of several gross human categories. At the beginning of this book, it was stated that tracking is an educational response to the increased pupil diversity created by pressure on adolescents from employers, parents, and educators themselves to stay in school longer. While the track system may be an efficient way to screen large numbers of youth from the upper levels of educational and economic systems, and while it may be a bureaucratic convenience, tracking is crude at best and destructive at worst in psychological and educational terms. Predictably, the occupants of the categories created by tracking come to be perceived, treated, and taught according to what they are thought to be, in common with others in the category: college material or not college material, bright or not bright, motivated or not motivated, fast or not fast. Yet psychologists of individual differences and learning have been saying for years what every parent already knows from common sense and experience: each child is unique in aptitudes, style of interaction, learning style and rate, energy level, interests, self-attitudes, reactions to challenge and stress, and countless other ways. New educational environments must be adaptable to these differences.

The second principle is that the potential for individual growth and development is virtually unlimited and must be freed and stimulated to develop as fully as possible during each person's lifetime. We must stop assuming that human potential is somehow fixed or circumscribed. Tragically, tracking—and indeed the whole structure of schooling—is founded on this premise. As one commentator put it, ". . . the task of *preventing* the new generation from changing in any deep or significant way is precisely what most societies require of their educators" (Leonard, 1968, p. 7). Not surprisingly, then:

> The most obvious barrier between our children and the kind of education that can free their enormous potential seems to be the educational system itself: a vast, suffocating web of people, practices, and presumptions, kindly in intent, ponderous in response (Leonard, 1968, p. 101).

In building new environments for becoming—with rich and limitless opportunities for exploration into self and other people, other places, times, ideas, and the unknown—educators can play a part in seeing to it that more than today's mere fraction of potential learning and growing is unleashed.

The third principle is that "education, at best, is ecstatic" (Leonard, 1968, p. 20). For the non-college-bound—indeed for the vast majority, including neat and tidy high-achievers—"schooling" (we can hardly call it "learning") is the very opposite:

> A visitor from another planet might conclude that our schools are hell-bent on creating—in a society that offers leisure and demands creativity—a generation of joyless drudges. . . . when joy is absent, the effectiveness of the learning process falls and falls until the human being is operating hesitantly, grudgingly, fearfully at only a tiny fraction of his potential (Leonard, 1968, pp. 7, 20).

For joy to enter learning, "cognitive learning" must be reunited with affective, physical, and behavioral growth. Moreover, new student roles must be created which provide for learning through active, productive behavior. At present, unfortunately, students on all tracks must endure day after day of externally imposed, passive, reactive behavior. It is commonly assumed that, having gone through the motions of being filled up like receptacles with "facts" and "knowledge" for a specified period of time, students will then be ready to begin active, productive living. By playing the game of passivity, by listening all the while to what "life" will be like later on, adolescents are expected to end up prepared to be creative, responsible adults.

However, more and more students are saying that the payoff must be now as well as later, that they are tired of being inactive, of always consuming but never producing. In short, they want education to be satisfying and fulfilling. If new educational environments are developed in response to this plea, will learning then stop with a diploma —or even before? Or might not learning become something to delight in, to seek after, to carry on as a central interest throughout life?

New learning-teaching-living environments must begin with these simple principles, not only to eliminate the negative effects of tracking, but also to avoid several features of the student role that alienate all types of students: passivity, pervasive subordination, forced separation from self, fragmented and stultifying sequencing of learning, age segregation, isolation from community life (with the consequent unrealities of school life), and an almost exclusive emphasis on instrumentalism, postponement of gratification, and the future as opposed to payoff from schooling in the present.[1]

If schools are to develop new environments that will generate more satisfying and fulfilling experiences of learning and personal development for each student, then teachers, administrators, and policy makers must shift their conception about education's main mission from *educational and occupational selection* to humanistic and individualistic *personal development*. The schools must no longer be viewed principally as agents of the technocratic society,[2] functioning through tracking and other means to screen out at an early age those judged not to be "college (that is, white-collar) material" as well as to acculturate all students to the existing economic, technological, and political order. While education must provide the expertise and knowledge base needed for the operation and progressive develop-

[1]For a discussion of how these features of the student role are likely to contribute to student alienation, see Schafer (1970).

[2]For an excellent discussion of the technocratic society and its youthful opposition, see Roszak (1969).

ment of society, it can best do this by unleashing the potential and promise of each person:

> . . . the highly interactive, regenerative technological society now emerging will work best, indeed will *require* something akin to mass genius, mass creativity, and lifelong learning (Leonard, 1968, p. 115).

APPROACHES TO CHANGE

Thus far the discussion of the implications of this study has pointed out the need to develop new models of learning and living as alternatives to tracking—in fact, to schooling as it is now known. Several guidelines or principles for new models have been identified, but specific learning structures have been deliberately shunned as an answer to the question: What will work? The decision to pose only general principles stems from the fact that neither educators nor behavioral scientists really know much about learning and other developmental outcomes of specific alternative models. (The data of this study suggest what is wrong with track systems, but not what alternatives are best.) There is growing awareness, however, that fundamentally new environments must be developed.

Two approaches must be simultaneously pursued, one within the structure of the schools, one outside. First, it is clear that for a long time to come, most children and adolescents will attend public schools. Therefore, new and imaginative efforts must be made to develop humanistic and equalitarian models within that framework. Such environments must be carefully planned and evaluated, so that they will be based on recent evidence and thinking about learning and not coopted by the traditions and pressures of the host institution, and so that new knowledge can be systematically developed about what models are most effective. The most promising model for this kind of experimentation and development is what has come to be known as "experimental social innovation." A compelling case for this approach is made in the following:

> There is an urgent need for society to create procedures that will bring about social change in a systematic, orderly, and rational manner. To accomplish this, however, information concerning the outcomes of possible alternative solutions to any given social problem must be obtained and disseminated to legislators and other decision-makers before a particular solution is adopted. This is necessary because once a solution is adopted and codified through legislation, the possibility of change in the solution is much more difficult. Ideally, procedures for social change should be organized to create in a society the readiness to meet new conditions; they should also specify how to

test alternative solutions to social problems. Alternative solutions to current social problems can be evaluated if a small and well-controlled model for each possible solution is implanted in the community and rigorously investigated. But these model social subsystems cannot be established and, in turn, compared, unless a research methodology is created for this precise purpose. Such experimental procedures have certain unique characteristics that differentiate them from other research procedures used in naturalistic social action studies, laboratory experiments, surveys, and social action service programs (Fairweather, 1967, p. 4).

Fairweather's descriptions of the process and results of experimental social innovations in mental hospitals should prove useful in guiding the application of this model of change to schools (Fairweather *et al.*, 1969). Just as Fairweather tested models of mental institutions outside existing hospitals, it is vital that public schools also develop and test entirely new, independent learning environments.

Second, it is vital that alternatives to public schools be planned and tested (Schafer and Knapp, 1968) at the same time that efforts are made to effect fundamental reforms within the framework of public education.[3] This is already happening:

Many parents and teachers have begun to see for themselves the boredom, fear, and grievous lack of learning that too often accompany schooling—not only for the poor and the black, but for suburban white youngsters as well—and they have begun to ask what can be done about it.

The revolt is no longer against outdated curriculums or ineffective teaching methods—the concerns of the late Fifties and early Sixties. The revolt today is against the institution itself, against the implicit assumption that learning must be imposed on children by adults, that learning is not something one does for himself, but something designated by a teacher. Schools operating on this assumption tend to hold children in a prolonged state of dependency, to keep them from discovering their own capacities for learning, and to encourage a sense of impotence and lack of worth. The search is for alternatives to this kind of institution.

In the past two years, increasing numbers of parents and teachers have struck out on their own to develop a new kind of school that will allow a new kind of education, that will create independent, courageous people able to face and deal with the shifting complexities of the modern world. The new

[3]According to *Saturday Review* (June 25, 1970), several excellent sources of information about free schools are available: *New Schools Exchange* (2840 Hidden Valley Lane, Santa Barbara, Calif. 93103); Constance Woulf, *The Free Learner* (4615 Canyon Road, El Sobrante, Calif. 94803); *New Schools Manual* (New Directions Community School, 445 Tenth St., Richmond, Calif. 94801); *The Big Rock Candy Mountain* (Portola Institute, Inc., 1115 Merrill St., Menlo Park, Calif. 94025); *Directory of Free Schools* (Alternatives Foundation, 1526 Gravenstein Highway, Sebastopol, Calif. 97452); *A Bibliography for the Free School Movement* (Summerhill Society, 339 Lafayette St., New York, N. Y. 10012).

schools, or free schools, or community schools—they go by all these names—have sprung up by the hundreds across the country (Stretch, 1970, p. 76).

If the movement toward alternative schools is to be a step forward, it is imperative that a humanistic vision be combined with sound planning, based on the most advanced thinking about how learning and personal development are affected by educational environments. The relatively high attrition rate among experimental schools stems in part from the fact that would-be radical educators fail to anticipate the huge step from ideology and ideals to the nitty-gritty of how an effective learning environment for implementing those ideals ought to operate (Stretch, 1970). Hopefully, behavioral scientists will be useful in helping shape new, more effective models.

Just as with reforms within the public schools, radical, alternative private schools must be carefully evaluated as well as planned. To be sure, the notion of quantifying and measuring learning outcomes is distasteful to many of the very people interested in developing experimental schools. Yet the fact remains that most learning outcomes can be measured and must be assessed and compared among different types of learning environments if the alternative-school movement is to avoid falling into the same trap as today's public schools—blindly perpetuating and defending ineffectual education.

The lack of financial support is the greatest impediment facing the experimental-school movement. It is imperative that the federal government assume a greater share of this responsibility. As many have suggested, alternative schools could and should be supported by a variety of public agencies and by private foundations, labor unions, industries, and other organizations which are sharing the riches of the affluent society (K. Clark, 1968).

Whether through drastically reformed existing schools or alternative learning environments, education must afford a chance for every student to experience an individualized, mind-expanding, joy-producing educational process, based on equality of opportunity. But it must do even more. Education must, in the final analysis, address itself to the vital issues of man and his survival. Educators then can take a long step toward preserving life itself:

"Right answers," specialization, standardization, narrow competition, eager acquisition, aggression, detachment from the self. Without them, it has seemed, the social machinery would break down. Do not call the schools cruel or unnatural for furthering what society has demanded. The reason we need radical reform in education is that society's demands are changing radically. It is quite safe to say that the human characteristics now being inculcated will not work much longer. Already they are not only inappropriate, but destructive. If education continues along the old tack, humanity sooner or later will simply destroy itself (Leonard, 1968, p. 124).

We must begin now.

References

Abelson, Robert P., *et al. Theories of Cognitive Consistency.* Chicago: Rand McNally, 1968.

Alexander, C. Norman, Jr., and Ernest Q. Campbell. "Peer Influences on Adolescent Educational Aspirations and Attainments," *American Sociological Review*, 29 (1964), 568–575.

Anderson, Theodore R., and Morris Zelditch, Jr. *A Basic Course in Statistics.* New York: Holt, Rinehart and Winston, 1968.

Backman, Carl W., and Paul F. Secord. *A Social Psychological View of Education.* New York: Harcourt Brace Jovanovich, 1968.

Becker, Howard S. *Outsiders: Studies in the Sociology of Deviance.* New York: Free Press, 1963.

Becker, Howard S., ed., *The Other Side: Perspectives on Deviance.* Glencoe, Ill.: Free Press, 1964.

Borg, W. R. *Ability Grouping in the Public Schools.* Madison, Wis.: Dembar Educational Research Services, 1966.

Brookover, Wilbur B., and David Gottlieb. *A Sociology of Education.* 2nd ed.; New York: American Book, 1964.

Campbell, Ernest Q., and C. Norman Alexander, Jr. "Structural Effects and Interpersonal Relations," *American Journal of Sociology*, 71 (1965), 284–289.

Cicourel, Aaron V., and John I. Kitsuse. *The Educational Decision-Makers.* Indianapolis: Bobbs-Merrill, 1963.

Clark, Burton R. *Educating the Expert Society.* Scranton: Chandler Publishing Company, 1962.

Clark, Kenneth. "Alternative Public School Systems," *Harvard Educational Review*, 38 (1968), 100–113.

Clark, Kenneth. "Educational Stimulation of Racially Disadvantaged Children," in Harry A. Passow, ed., *Education in Depressed Areas.* New York: Teachers College Press, Columbia University, 1963. Pp. 142–162.

Cohen, Albert K. *Delinquent Boys.* Glencoe, Ill.: Free Press, 1955.

Coleman, James S. *The Adolescent Society.* New York: Free Press, 1961.

Coleman, James S. *Adolescents and the Schools.* New York: Basic Books, 1965.

Coleman, James S., *et al. Equality of Educational Opportunity.* Washington, D.C.: Government Printing Office, 1966.

Committee on Education and Labor of the United States House of Representatives. *A Task Force Study of the Public School System in the District of Columbia as it Relates to the War on Poverty.* Washington, D.C.: Government Printing Office, 1966.

Conant, James B. *The Comprehensive High School.* New York: McGraw-Hill, 1967.

Conant, James B. *Slums and Schools.* New York: McGraw-Hill, 1961.

Curriculum Survey Committee. *Report.* San Francisco: Board of Education, San Francisco Unified School District, April 1960.

Dahrendorf, Ralf. *Class and Class Conflict in Industrial Society*. Stanford, Calif.: Stanford University Press, 1959.

Douglas, J. W. B. *The Home and the School*. London: MacGibbon and Kee, 1964.

Douglas, J. W. B. "Streaming by Ability," *New Society*, 3 (1964), 6–7.

Dyer, Henry S. "Social Factors and Equal Educational Opportunity," *Harvard Educational Review*, 38 (1968), 38–56.

Elder, Glen H., Jr. "Life Opportunity and Personality: Some Consequences of Stratified Secondary Education in Great Britain," *Sociology of Education*, 38 (1965), 173–202.

Erickson, Kai. "Notes on the Sociology of Deviance," in Howard S. Becker, ed., *The Other Side: Perspectives on Deviance*. Glencoe, Ill.: Free Press, 1964. Pp. 9–21.

Examiner's Manual: California Short-Form Test of Mental Maturity. Monterey: California Test Bureau, 1963.

Examiner's Manual: The Lorge-Thorndike Intelligence Tests. Boston: Houghton Mifflin, 1957.

Fairweather, George W. *Methods of Experimental Social Innovation*. New York: Wiley, 1967.

Fairweather, George W., ed. *Social Psychology in Treating Mental Illness: An Experimental Approach*. New York: Wiley, 1964.

Fairweather, George W., *et al. Community Life for the Mentally Ill: An Alternative to Institutional Care*. Chicago: Aldine, 1969.

Fantini, Mario D., and Gerald Weinstein. *The Disadvantaged: Challenge to Education*. New York: Harper and Row, 1968.

Festinger, Leon. *Conflict, Decision, and Dissonance*. Stanford, Calif.: Stanford University Press, 1964.

Festinger, Leon. *A Theory of Cognitive Dissonance*. Evanston, Ill.: Row, Peterson, 1957.

Folger, John K., and Charles B. Nam. *Education of the American Population*. 1960 Census Monograph; Washington, D.C.: Government Printing Office, 1967.

Frankel, Edward. "The Comprehensive High School," *Urban Review*, 2 (1968), 20–31.

Frankel, Edward. *The Four Year Comprehensive High School*. New York: Center for Urban Education, August 1966.

Frease, Dean. *The Schools, Self-Concept, and Delinquency*. Unpublished doctoral dissertation, University of Oregon, 1969.

Friedenberg, Edgar. *The Dignity of Youth and Other Atavisms*. Boston: Beacon Press, 1965.

Glasser, William. *Schools Without Failure*. New York: Harper and Row, 1969.

Goldberg, Marian L, Harry A. Passow, and Joseph Justman. *The Effects of Ability Grouping*. New York: Teachers College Press, Columbia University, 1966.

Goodman, Paul. *Compulsory Mis-education*. New York: Vintage Books, 1962.

Hahn, Walter. "Does the Comprehensive High School Have a Culture in Europe?" *Journal of Secondary Education*, 42 (1967), 86–93.

Haller, Archibald O., and C. E. Butterworth. "Peer Influences on Levels of Occupational and Educational Aspirations," *Social Forces*, 38 (1960), 289–295.

Hansen, Carl F. *The Four-Track Curriculum*. Englewood Cliffs, N.J.: Prentice-Hall, 1964.

Hargreaves, David H. *Social Relations in a Secondary School*. New York: Humanities Press, 1967.

Hobson v. Hansen. 269 F. Supp. 401 (1967). Washington, D.C.: Government Printing Office.

Jackson, Brian. *Streaming: An Education System in Miniature*. London: Routledge and Kegan Paul, 1964.

Katz, Daniel, and Robert L. Kahn. *Social Psychology of Organizations*. New York: Wiley, 1966.

Keller, F. J. *The Comprehensive High School*. New York: Harper and Brothers, 1955.

Kelly, Delos Harwill. *Social Class, School Status, and Self-Evaluation as Related to Adolescent Values, Success, and Deviance*. Unpublished doctoral dissertation, University of Oregon, 1970.

Leonard, George B. *Education and Ecstasy*. New York: Dell, 1968.

Levine, Daniel U. "Whatever Happened to the Ideal of the Comprehensive High School?" *Phi Delta Kappan*, 48 (1966), 62–64.

McDill, E. L., and James S. Coleman. "Family and Peer Influences in College Plans of High School Students," *Sociology of Education*, 38 (1965), 112–126.

McDill, E. L., and James S. Coleman. "High School Social Status, College Plans, and Interest in Academic Achievement: A Panel Analysis," *American Sociological Review*, 28 (1963), 905–918.

Mallery, David. *High School Students Speak Out*. New York: Harper and Brothers, 1962.

Mead, Margaret. *Culture and Commitment: A Study of the Generation Gap*. New York: Doubleday, 1970.

Mendelson, Wallace. *Discrimination*. Englewood Cliffs, N.J.: Prentice-Hall, 1962.

Pearl, Arthur. "Slim and None—the Poor's Two Chances," in Daniel Schreiber, ed., *Profile of the School Dropout*. New York: Vintage Books, 1967. Pp. 313–327.

Pearl, Arthur. "Youth in Lower Class Settings," in Muzafer Sherif and Carolyn W. Sherif, eds., *Problems of Youth*. Chicago: Aldine, 1965. Pp. 89–109.

Pearl, Arthur, and Frank Reissman. *New Careers for the Poor*. New York: Free Press, 1965.

Peterson, Leroy J., Richard A. Rossmiller, and Marlin M. Volz. *The Law and Public School Operation*. New York: Harper and Row, 1969.

Pounds, Ralph L., and James R. Bryner. *The School in American Society*. New York: Macmillan, 1967.

Ravitz, Mel. "The Role of the School in the Urban Setting," in Harry A. Passow, ed., *Education in Depressed Areas*. New York: Teachers College Press, Columbia University, 1963. Pp. 6–23.

Rehberg, Richard A., and Walter E. Schafer. "Participation in Interscholastic Athletics and College Expectations," *American Journal of Sociology*, 73 (1968), 732–740.

Rosenthal, Robert, and Lenore Jacobson. *Pygmalion in the Classroom.* New York: Holt, Rinehart and Winston, 1968.

Roszak, Theodore. *The Making of a Counter Culture: Reflections on the Technocratic Society and its Youthful Opposition*. Garden City, N.Y.: Anchor Books, 1969.

Sarri, Rosemary C., and Robert D. Vinter. "Group Work for the Control of Behavior Problems in Secondary Schools," in David Street, ed., *Innovation in Mass Education*. New York: Wiley, 1969. Pp. 91–119.

Schafer, Walter E. "Crisis, Change and Evaluative Research," *Oregon Education*, 44 (1970), 22–24, 32.

Schafer, Walter E. "Deviance in the Public Schools: An Interactional View," in Edwin J. Thomas, ed., *Behavioral Science for Social Workers*. New York: Free Press, 1967. Pp. 51–58.

Schafer, Walter E. *Student Careers in Two Public High Schools*. Unpublished doctoral dissertation, University of Michigan, 1965.

Schafer, Walter E., and J. Michael Armer. "Athletes Are Not Inferior Students," *Trans-action*, 6 (1968), 21–26.

Schafer, Walter E., and J. Michael Armer. "High School Curriculum Placement: A Study of Educational Selection." Paper presented at annual meeting of Pacific Sociological Association, Vancouver, B.C., 1966.

Schafer, Walter E., and Daniel Knapp. *Delinquency Prevention Through Education.* Washington, D.C.: United States Department of Health, Education and Welfare, Youth Development and Delinquency Prevention Administration, 1968.

Schafer, Walter E., and Kenneth Polk. "Delinquency and the Schools," in President's Commission on Law Enforcement and Administration of Justice, *Task Force Report: Juvenile Delinquency and Youth Crime.* Washington, D.C.: Government Printing Office, 1967. Pp. 222–277.

Schrag, Peter. "Growing Up on Mechanic Street," *Saturday Review*, 53 (1970), 59–61, 78–79.

Sexton, Patricia Cayo. *The American School: A Sociological Analysis.* Englewood Cliffs, N.J.: Prentice-Hall, 1967.

Sexton, Patricia Cayo. *Education and Income: Inequality of Opportunity in the Public Schools*. New York: Viking Press, 1961.

Shores, J. H. "What Does Research Say About Ability Grouping by Class?" *Illinois Education*, 53 (1964), 169–172.

Snyder, Eldon E. "A Longitudinal Analysis of the Relationships Between High School Student Values, Social Participation, and Educational-Occupational Achievement," *Sociology of Education*, 42 (1969), 261–270.

Spady, William G. "Lament for the Letterman: Effects of Peer Status and Extracurricular Activities on Goals and Achievement," *American Journal of Sociology*, 75 (1970), 680–702.

Stinchcombe, Arthur. *Rebellion in a High School*. Chicago: Quadrangle, 1964.

Stouffer, Samuel A. "The Student-Problems Related to the Use of Academic Ability," *The Identification and Education of the Academically Talented Student in the American Secondary School*. NEA Conference Report,

February 1958. Cited in Patricia Cayo Sexton, *Education and Income: Inequality of Opportunity in the Public Schools.* New York: Viking Press, 1961.

Stretch, Bonnie Barrett. "The Rise of the Free School," *Saturday Review*, 53 (1970), 76–79.

Tanner, Daniel. *Schools for Youth: Change and Challenge in Secondary Education.* New York: Macmillan, 1965.

"Teacher Opinion Poll," *NEA Journal*, 57 (1968), 53.

Thelen, Herbert A. *Classroom Grouping for Teachability.* New York: Wiley, 1967.

Thomas, R. Murray, and Shirley M. Thomas. *Individual Differences in the Classroom.* New York: David McKay, 1965.

Tillman, R., and J. H. Hull. "Is Ability Grouping Taking Schools in the Wrong Direction?" *Nation's Schools*, 73 (1964), 70–71, 128–129.

Tree, Cristina. "Grouping Pupils in New York City," *Urban Review*, 3 (1968), 8–15.

Turner, Ralph. "Contest and Sponsored Mobility," *American Sociological Review*, 25 (1960), 855–867.

United States Commission on Civil Rights. *Racial Isolation in the Public Schools.* Washington, D.C.: Government Printing Office, 1968.

United States Office of Education. *Digest of Educational Statistics.* Washington, D.C.: Government Printing Office, 1969.

Venn, Grant. *Man, Education and Work.* Washington, D.C.: American Council on Education, 1964.

Vinter, Robert D., and Rosemary C. Sarri. "Malperformance in the Public School: A Group Work Approach," *Social Work*, 10 (1965), 3–13.

Warner, W. Lloyd, Robert J. Havighurst, and M. B. Loeb. *Who Shall Be Educated?* New York: Harper and Row, 1944.

Werthman, Carl. "The Function of Social Definitions in the Development of Delinquent Careers," in President's Commission on Law Enforcement and Administration of Justice, *Task Force Report: Juvenile Delinquency and Youth Crime.* Washington, D.C.: Government Printing Office, 1967. Pp. 155–170.

Westby-Gibson, Dorothy. *Grouping Students for Improved Instruction.* Englewood Cliffs, N.J.: Prentice-Hall, 1966.

Youth in the Ghetto. New York: Harlem Youth Opportunities Unlimited, Inc., 1964.

Appendix: Tables

TABLE I. DISTRIBUTION BETWEEN TRACKS BY FATHER'S OCCUPATION, CONTROLLING FOR IQ AND PREVIOUS ACHIEVEMENT, %

	College-Prep	*Non-College-Prep*	*Total*	*N*
High IQ				
High previous achievement				
White-collar	92	8	100	(214)
Blue-collar	63	37	100	(150)
Low previous achievement				
White-collar	90	10	100	(95)
Blue-collar	53	47	100	(64)
Low IQ				
High previous achievement				
White-collar	88	12	100	(85)
Blue-collar	62	38	100	(60)
Low previous achievement				
White-collar	64	36	100	(175)
Blue-collar	33	67	100	(222)

TABLE II. DISTRIBUTION BETWEEN TRACKS BY RACE, CONTROLLING FOR IQ AND PREVIOUS ACHIEVEMENT, %

	College-Prep	*Non-College-Prep*	*Total*	*N*
High IQ				
High previous achievement				
White	82	18	100	(352)
Black	40	60	100	(25)
Low previous achievement				
White	75	25	100	(156)
Black	(3)	(6)		(9)
Low IQ				
High previous achievement				
White	81	19	100	(122)
Black	54	46	100	(24)
Low previous achievement				
White	53	47	100	(336)
Black	18	82	100	(74)

TABLE III. DIFFERENCES BETWEEN TRACKS IN ACADEMIC ACHIEVEMENT, CONTROLLING FOR FATHER'S OCCUPATION, IQ, AND PREVIOUS ACHIEVEMENT, %

	High	*High Average*	*Low Average*	*Low*	*Total*	*N*
White-collar						
High IQ						
High previous achievement						
College-prep	58	28	12	2	100	(197)
Non-college-prep	6	29	41	24	100	(17)
Low previous achievement						
College-prep	34	26	26	15	101	(86)
Non-college-prep	(0)	(0)	(4)	(5)		(9)
Low IQ						
High previous achievement						
College-prep	41	28	23	8	100	(75)
Non-college-prep	(0)	(1)	(8)	(1)		(10)
Low previous achievement						
College-prep	28	31	25	15	99	(111)
Non-college-prep	2	8	37	53	100	(64)
Blue-collar						
High IQ						
High previous achievement						
College-prep	40	36	17	7	100	(95)
Non-college-prep	1	29	25	45	100	(45)
Low previous achievement						
College-prep	11	31	32	26	100	(34)
Non-college-prep	11	17	24	48	100	(30)
Low IQ						
High previous achievement						
College-prep	14	32	40	14	100	(37)
Non-college-prep	4	32	41	22	99	(23)
Low previous achievement						
College-prep	20	29	29	21	99	(75)
Non-college-prep	2	17	23	58	100	(147)

TABLE IV. DIFFERENCES BETWEEN TRACKS IN ACADEMIC ACHIEVEMENT, CONTROLLING FOR SEX, %

	High	*High Average*	*Low Average*	*Low*	*Total*	*N*
Boys						
College-prep	29	28	27	17	101	(370)
Non-college-prep	1	15	28	56	100	(225)
Girls						
College-prep	46	31	18	6	101	(382)
Non-college-prep	4	20	34	42	100	(180)

TABLE V. DIFFERENCES BETWEEN TRACKS IN EXTRACURRICULAR PARTICIPATION, CONTROLLING FOR FATHER'S OCCUPATION, IQ, AND PREVIOUS ACHIEVEMENT, %

	Three or More Activities	*One or Two Activities*	*No Activities*	*Total*	*N*
White-collar					
High IQ					
High previous achievement					
College-prep	55	35	10	100	(168)
Non-college-prep	(2)	(3)	(5)		(10)
Low previous achievement					
College-prep	40	26	34	100	(76)
Non-college-prep	(1)	(3)	(2)		(6)
Low IQ					
High previous achievement					
College-prep	48	37	15	100	(59)
Non-college-prep	(1)	(3)	(2)		(6)
Low previous achievement					
College-prep	41	39	20	100	(85)
Non-college-prep	12	33	55	100	(49)
Blue-collar					
High IQ					
High previous achievement					
College-prep	39	44	17	100	(41)
Non-college-prep	9	27	64	100	(22)
Low previous achievement					
College-prep	(6)	(4)	(3)		(13)
Non-college-prep	(0)	(5)	(7)		(12)
Low IQ					
High previous achievement					
College-prep	35	35	30	100	(26)
Non-college-prep	(2)	(4)	(1)		(7)
Low previous achievement					
College-prep	22	32	46	100	(43)
Non-college-prep	10	25	65	100	(87)

TABLE VI. DIFFERENCES BETWEEN TRACKS IN EXTRACURRICULAR PARTICIPATION, CONTROLLING FOR SEX, %

	Three or More Activities	*One or Two Activities*	*No Activities*	*Total*	*N*
Boys					
College-prep	42	35	23	100	(274)
Non-college-prep	9	32	59	100	(132)
Girls					
College-prep	46	34	20	100	(263)
Non-college-prep	13	29	58	100	(84)

Table VII. Differences between Tracks in Dropout Rate, Controlling for Father's Occupation, IQ, and Previous Achievement, %

	Graduated	*Transferred*	*Dropped Out*	*Total*	*N*
White-collar					
High IQ					
High previous achievement					
College-prep	93	7	0	100	(197)
Non-college-prep	93	0	7	101	(17)
Low previous achievement					
College-prep	72	24	4	100	(86)
Non-college-prep	(9)	(0)	(0)		(9)
Low IQ					
High previous achievement					
College-prep	89	8	3	100	(75)
Non-college-prep	(9)	(1)	(0)		(10)
Low previous achievement					
College-prep	80	17	3	100	(111)
Non-college-prep	48	11	41	100	(64)
Blue-collar					
High IQ					
High previous achievement					
College-prep	85	10	5	100	(95)
Non-college-prep	87	11	2	100	(55)
Low previous achievement					
College-prep	71	18	11	100	(34)
Non-college-prep	69	4	27	100	(30)
Low IQ					
High previous achievement					
College-prep	82	7	11	100	(37)
Non-college-prep	83	4	13	101	(23)
Low previous achievement					
College-prep	82	14	4	100	(75)
Non-college-prep	51	5	44	100	(147)

TABLE VIII. DIFFERENCES BETWEEN TRACKS IN DROPOUT RATE, CONTROLLING FOR SEX, %

	Graduated	*Transferred*	*Dropped Out*	*Total*	*N*
Boys					
College-prep	85	10	5	100	(370)
Non-college-prep	54	8	38	100	(225)
Girls					
College-prep	90	7	3	100	(382)
Non-college-prep	53	14	33	100	(180)

TABLE IX. DIFFERENCES BETWEEN TRACKS IN DELINQUENCY RATE, CONTROLLING FOR FATHER'S OCCUPATION, IQ, AND PREVIOUS ACHIEVEMENT, %

	Non-delinquent	*Delinquent*	*Total*	*N*
White-collar				
High IQ				
High previous achievement				
College-prep	96	4	100	(197)
Non-college-prep	94	6	100	(17)
Low previous achievement				
College-prep	92	8	100	(86)
Non-college-prep	(8)	(1)		(9)
Low IQ				
High previous achievement				
College-prep	96	4	100	(75)
Non-college-prep	(10)	(0)		(10)
Low previous achievement				
College-prep	94	6	100	(111)
Non-college-prep	84	16	100	(64)
Blue-collar				
High IQ				
High previous achievement				
College-prep	97	3	100	(95)
Non-college-prep	80	20	100	(55)
Low previous achievement				
College-prep	94	6	100	(31)
Non-college-prep	86	14	100	(30)
Low IQ				
High previous achievement				
College-prep	87	13	100	(38)
Non-college-prep	95	5	100	(22)
Low previous achievement				
College-prep	91	9	100	(75)
Non-college-prep	82	18	100	(147)

TABLE X. DIFFERENCES BETWEEN TRACKS IN DELINQUENCY RATE, CONTROLLING FOR SEX, %

	Nondelinquent	*Delinquent*	*Total*	*N*
Boys				
College-prep	93	7	100	(370)
Non-college-prep	82	18	100	(225)
Girls				
College-prep	95	5	100	(382)
Non-college-prep	88	12	100	(180)

Index